THE AI EMPIRE BUILDER BLUEPRINT

A Complete Woman's Guide to Building a Million-Dollar Empire with AI

By Sarah Melland

Contents

INTRODUCTION

A Personal Letter From Sarah

Every empire starts with a woman who got tired.
Tired of guessing.
Tired of struggling.
Tired of shrinking her brilliance to make other people comfortable.
Tired of waiting for permission, timing, validation, or the "right idea."

This book was born from the moment I realized something earth-shattering: **we are not confused, we are conditioned.** Conditioned to play small. Conditioned to distrust our own genius. Conditioned to believe money is made through suffering, burnout, and self-abandonment.

But the truth is this:

Money responds to identity.
Wealth responds to alignment.
Success responds to the woman you become, long before it responds to the business you build.

THE AI Empire Blueprint

I didn't build this blueprint from theory.
I built it from survival.
From starting over.
From rebuilding myself when life fell apart.
From using AI as the one thing that could keep up with the speed of my ideas, my ambition, and the size of the life I knew I was meant for.

I'm not teaching you how to hustle. I'm teaching you how to **come home to yourself** and use AI as a mirror, an accelerator, and a strategy partner that reflects back your power so you can finally build wealth the way women were *meant* to: with clarity, ease, alignment, and emotional safety.

This isn't a business book. This is a **rebuild-your-identity-at-the-quantum-level** book.

Step by step, you're going to:
- shift your subconscious money story
- activate the wealthy identity you've been avoiding
- discover your purpose and pattern-based calling
- generate 100+ aligned business ideas
- build your first offers
- map your signature empire
- architect a million-dollar digital ecosystem
- become the woman money trusts, responds to, and follows

I'm not here to give you "motivation."
I'm here to give you **structure**, **identity**, and a **blueprint** rooted in the psychology of wealth, the energetics of expansion, and the power of AI as your personal strategist.

Everything in this book is designed to unlock the version of you who already exists, the one you keep pretending isn't ready.

By the time you finish, you won't just know what business to build…
You'll finally understand **why you're the woman built to lead it.**

Turn the page, my love.

Your empire is already forming.
Let's build it.

ABOUT THE CHAOTIC MIND

Who I Am & Why I'm an Expert at This

I'm Sarah Melland, writer, strategist, identity architect, and the creator behind dozens of digital brands, games, books, and multimillion-dollar micro-business ecosystems. I specialize in turning a woman's lived experience into a profitable online empire not through hustle, but through psychology, pattern recognition, and AI-powered clarity.

I've built entire brands from scratch with no investors, no ads, and no connections using nothing but strategy, creativity, identity work, and AI. I've created viral online products, bestselling digital assets, and niche websites that scaled from ideas to income. I've helped countless women find the business that feels like THEM instead of forcing themselves into something suffocating.

My genius is simple:
I see patterns other people miss.
I turn chaos into clarity.
I use AI the way it was meant to be used not as a tool, but as a **partner** in identity transformation, business architecture, and wealth creation.

I built this blueprint because I know what it feels like to rebuild your life from the ground up, to refuse to stay small, and to build success on your own terms.

Everything in this book is the system I wish I had when I was beginning. The system that turns your purpose, your personality, your energy, your strengths, and your truth into a business model that actually makes sense.

I've lived every single step you're about to take.
And now I'm handing you the map.

You're not here to build a business.
You're here to build an empire. the one that finally feels like you.

STEP 1:

WEALTH & SUCCESS MINDSET PROMPTS

"Prompts to Shift Into a Wealth Identity Before You Build Your Empire"

Money responds to identity long before it responds to strategy.

This workbook is your first step in building an empire not because money comes first, but because **your mind does**. Before the ideas, before the brand, before the business plan, there is *you*: your beliefs, your capacity, your self-permission, and the way you've been secretly trained to think about wealth.

This is where we unwind the limits you inherited.
This is where we stop playing small.
This is where the wealthy version of you gets the microphone.

The woman who thrives isn't lucky. She's aligned.

This workbook will help you use AI not as a crutch, but as a mirror, a reflection of the wealth already coded inside you. Let's shift your internal world so everything external can finally catch up.

HOW TO USE THIS STEP

AI is not here to tell you what to do. It's here to **show you the parts of yourself you've ignored**. Use it like a mentor, strategist, therapist, and future-you all-in-one.

How to interact with the prompts:

1. Pick a prompt from any section.
2. Type it directly into AI (ChatGPT).
3. Ask AI to answer as your highest, wealthiest, most successful future self.
4. Let the answer shift your perspective.
5. Integrate one action, one belief, or one thought immediately.

Best practices:

- Use 2–3 prompts each morning.
- Use deeper prompts when sabotaging or spiraling.
- Use the worksheets when you need clarity.
- Most importantly: Let the answers change you.

This workbook lays your foundation.
Everything else we build rests on this.

WEALTH IDENTITY ACTIVATION
(Guided Exercise)

Close your eyes. Imagine the wealthiest version of you.

Not the richest version you think you *should* be,
the richest version you *actually are*.

See her environment.
Her pace.
Her posture.
Her focus.
Her energy when she walks into a room.
How she solves problems.
How she receives money.
How she makes decisions without hesitation or guilt.

Now answer these:

1. What is she no longer willing to tolerate?

   _____

   _____

2. What emotional state does she refuse to make money decisions from?

   _____

   _____

3. What emotional state does she choose instead?

   _____

   _____

4. What belief does she hold that I don't... yet?

   _____

   _____

   _____

5. What is one daily habit she practices that I'm ready to adopt?

   _____

   _____

This visualization is not pretend.
It's memory from a future you're becoming.

IDENTITY PROMPTS

Identity prompts are designed to do two things:

1. Reveal who you're becoming.

(You ask AI as if it's your wealthiest future self.)

2. Reveal who you've been.

(You reflect in your own journal after you read the AI answer.)

This two-step method helps you see the version of you you're growing into AND the patterns you're ready to leave behind.

How to use them:

1. Copy the prompt and ask AI to answer "as the highest, wealthiest version of me."

2. Read the response slowly. Notice what feels true, scary, or exciting.

3. Write your own reflection underneath.

4. Integrate one small shift into your day.

Identity doesn't change by force.
It changes by truth, clarity, and alignment.

Let the wealthy version of you guide the way.

1. "Describe the identity of the wealthiest version of me."

   _____

   _____

2. "What beliefs does she hold about herself that I don't yet?"

   _____

   _____

3. "How does she view money compared to me?"

   _____

   _____

4. "What does she do differently on an ordinary Tuesday?"

   _____

   _____

5. "What does she say 'no' to instantly?"

_____

_____

6. "What behaviors has she completely outgrown?"

_____

_____

7. "What does she prioritize that I currently avoid?"

_____

_____

8. "How does she speak to herself?"

_____

_____

9. "How does she view risk, opportunity, and timing?"

_____

_____

10. "What patterns does she refuse to repeat?"

_____

_____

11. "How does she create emotional safety for herself?"

_____

_____

12. "How would she describe the woman I am right now?"

_____

_____

13. "What advice would she give me today?"

_____

_____

14. "What energy would she walk into the world with?"

_____

_____

15. "If she were in charge of my life today, what would she change first?"

_____

_____

TEACHING PAGE:
YOUR SUBCONSCIOUS MONEY STORY

Every money decision you make is shaped by a story you didn't consciously choose. Most people live inside the financial fears, scarcity beliefs, and survival habits of their parents, teachers, childhood culture, or first heartbreak.

Your subconscious money story determines:
- what you think you deserve
- what you're willing to receive
- how much pressure you need to feel "motivated"
- how much wealth feels "safe"
- how much success triggers self-sabotage

You are not rewriting numbers…
you're rewriting **identity, safety, and possibility**.

This page begins your rewrite.

SUBCONSCIOUS REWIRING PROMPTS

How to Use the Subconscious Rewiring Prompts

Your subconscious money story was formed long before you had any conscious say in it through childhood, survival, culture, relationships, and the emotional patterns you adopted to stay safe. These prompts are designed to help you work *with* the subconscious, not against it.

You'll use a **3-step method**:

STEP 1 — Ask AI to reveal the hidden pattern.

Copy the prompt and ask: **"Answer this as if you're analyzing the hidden beliefs, fears, and emotional patterns shaping my relationship with money."**

AI will surface blind spots you may never have noticed. This is where truth rises.

STEP 2 — Let the insight land.

Read slowly. Notice what feels:
- accurate
- triggering
- familiar
- uncomfortable
- relieving
- surprising

Your subconscious responds to recognition.
Awareness alone begins the rewiring.

STEP 3 — Rewrite the story in your own words.

After AI reveals the pattern, journal:
- *What part of this feels true?*
- *Where have I lived this story?*
- *What is the new belief I'm choosing instead?*
- *What action matches the new belief?*

Identity shifts through repetition, but transformation begins with one rewritten sentence.

These prompts help you excavate the past so you can finally build a future that isn't shaped by inherited fear.

Ask AI:

1. "What money beliefs did I inherit that aren't mine?"

2. "Which ones still control my behavior?"

3. "How has fear shaped my financial identity?"

4. "When did I first learn that money could disappear?"

5. "What does my subconscious think wealth will cost me?"

6. "What does it think wealth will fix?"

7. "Where do I recreate struggle because it feels familiar?"

8. "Where do I avoid ease because it feels unsafe?"

9. "What parts of my money story are rooted in someone else's wounds?"

10. "What new story would support the version of me I'm becoming?"

11. "Rewrite my old money story in one paragraph."

12. "Write my new money story as if I already lived it."

13. "What truth am I finally ready to accept?"

14. "What lie am I finally ready to release?"

15. "What identity am I done performing?"

WORKSHEET: OLD STORY → NEW STORY

OLD STORY I WAS TAUGHT ABOUT MONEY:
(Write freely.)

_____
_____
_____
_____
_____

HOW THIS STORY LIMITED MY LIFE:
(What you repeated, tolerated, avoided.)

_____
_____
_____
_____
_____

NEW STORY I'M CHOOSING:
(Future-you voice.)

_____
_____
_____
_____
_____

THE FIRST BEHAVIOR THAT MATCHES THIS NEW STORY:
(One shift.)

_____
_____
_____
_____
_____

MONEY BLOCKS YOU DIDN'T KNOW YOU HAD

These hidden patterns sabotage even smart, capable women:

- Feeling guilty for wanting more
- Associating wealth with selfishness
- Believing you must earn money through struggle
- Fearing that success will isolate you
- Feeling irresponsible when life becomes easy
- Overgiving to prove worth
- Shrinking around people who can't handle your expansion
- Feeling unsafe being seen
- Mistaking chaos for "normal"
- Thinking wealth will cost you your identity

Reflection Question: **Which of these hit you the hardest — and where did it come from?**

MONEY BLOCK BREAKTHROUGHS

How to Use the Money Block Breakthrough Prompts

Money blocks aren't logical, they're emotional. They form in the moments you felt unsafe, unsupported, overwhelmed, or out of control with money or responsibility. Most people try to "push through" their blocks, but blocks don't disappear through force.

They dissolve through **awareness, compassion, and rewiring.**

These prompts help you uncover:
- the beliefs you didn't know you were carrying
- the fears that drive your financial hesitation
- the identity you've been unconsciously protecting
- the patterns you repeat without noticing
- the emotional loyalty you have to struggle or scarcity

To get the deepest breakthrough, use these prompts with AI:

STEP 1 — Ask AI to identify the block.

Type the prompt into AI and add: **"Answer this as if you're revealing the core emotional block behind my financial patterns."**

AI will surface the *root cause*: the wound, moment, or belief you've been organized around.

STEP 2 — Sit with the truth before rushing to fix it.

Breakthroughs happen in the pause. Don't skip this.

Ask:
- *Where have I lived this pattern?*

- *What emotions come up reading this?*
- *What part of me is still loyal to this belief?*

Awareness itself is transformation.

STEP 3 — Rewrite the block into a new truth.

After AI reveals the block, ask:

"Rewrite this belief into a powerful truth that aligns with the woman I'm becoming."

Then write your own version underneath.

This is where your subconscious shifts identity.

_____
_____
_____
_____
_____

Money blocks don't make you weak. They make you human and ready to rise.

Ask AI:

1. "What block am I most loyal to and why?"

2. "What would happen if I outgrew this block?"

3. "What am I afraid ease will reveal?"

4. "Where do I sabotage momentum?"

5. "Where do I unconsciously choose the familiar struggle?"

6. "What does my fear think it's protecting me from?"

7. "What does my future self know that I don't?"

8. "What breakthroughs am I closer to than I realize?"

9. "What am I avoiding taking responsibility for?"

10. "What would happen if I stopped waiting?"

11. "What belief would collapse my old limits instantly?"

12. "What's the REAL reason money triggers me?"

13. "How do I recreate scarcity even when I'm stable?"

14. "What pattern am I truly done performing?"

15. "What part of me is ready to win?"

WEALTH FREQUENCY:
THE VIBRATION OF A RICH MIND

Wealth frequency isn't magic.
It's identity + behavior + environment.

You shift frequency by shifting:

- your pace
- your emotional state
- your self-talk
- your surroundings
- your habits
- your reaction to fear
- your standards
- your boundaries

Wealth comes to women who feel **safe, certain, and capable** in their bodies. This page helps you build that state intentionally.

WEALTH FREQUENCY PROMPTS

How to Use the Wealth Frequency Prompts

Wealth isn't just a number, it's a frequency. And frequency is nothing mystical. It's the emotional, mental, and behavioral state you spend the most time in. Your body broadcasts your identity before your words do.

Wealth frequency is shaped by:
- your nervous system
- your standards
- your boundaries
- the environment you allow
- the pace you move at
- the thoughts you rehearse
- the emotions you normalize

These prompts help you shift from survival energy to expansion energy, the state where wealth actually feels safe to enter your life. To get the deepest transformation, use these prompts with AI in a **state-change format**:

STEP 1 — Ask AI to read your current frequency.

Type the prompt into AI and add: **"Analyze this through the lens of my current wealth frequency where I'm aligned, where I'm blocked, and what energy I'm operating from."**

This reveals the emotional baseline you've been living in.

STEP 2 — Ask AI how to raise your frequency.

After AI answers, follow up with:

"Now answer as the wealthiest version of me. What frequency do *I* need to embody to match her?"

This shifts you out of your default identity and into your future identity.

STEP 3 — Anchor the new frequency into a micro-action.

Frequency is created through repetition, not intensity.

Each time you complete a prompt, ask:

"What is one tiny action I can take today that matches this frequency?"

One action.
One behavior.
One energetic upgrade.

This is how women build wealth from identity, not exhaustion.

Wealth is not something you chase.
It's something you rise into.

Ask AI:

1. "What activities raise my wealth frequency instantly?"

2. "What activities collapse it?"

3. "What emotional state creates my best decisions?"

4. "What environments make me feel expansive?"

5. "What environments make me shrink?"

6. "What habits signal to my brain that I'm valuable?"

7. "What habits signal that I'm not?"

8. "What boundaries would upgrade my self-worth?"

9. "How does the wealthy version of me regulate her nervous system?"

10. "What does abundance feel like in my body?"

11. "What does scarcity feel like?"

12. "What do I need to stop performing to feel powerful?"

13. "What would I do today if overflow was the assumption?"

14. "What decision am I avoiding because I know it will change everything?"

15. "What identity shift would raise my wealth frequency the fastest?"

THE DAILY WEALTH ALIGNMENT ROUTINE

Morning (5–10 minutes)
• Ask AI: "What is the wealthiest choice I can make today?"
• Visualize future-you making decisions calmly and confidently.
• Replace one scarcity thought with a wealthy reframe.

Afternoon (1–2 minutes)
• Check in: "Am I acting from fear, habit, or expansion?"
• Shift accordingly.

Evening (5 minutes)
• List 3 wealth-aligned decisions you made today.
• Ask AI: "What pattern did I break today without realizing it?"

Weekly
• Do one bold action.
• Do one scary-but-important financial move.

Consistency beats intensity.
Identity beats strategy.

CONFIDENCE & EXPANSION PROMPTS

How to Use the Confidence & Expansion Prompts

Confidence isn't a personality trait, it's a decision. And expansion isn't a mindset, it's a pattern of behavior. Confidence grows every time you act in alignment with your future self instead of your fear-based self. Expansion happens every time you stretch your identity past what feels familiar.

These prompts help you do both. They're designed to reveal:
- where you're shrinking
- where you're hesitating
- where you're playing small
- where you're rehearsing old limits
- where you're pretending to be less powerful than you are
- where you're sabotaging because you're afraid of your own potential

And most importantly…

They help you see the **version of you who is ready to lead**.

Use these prompts with AI when you're ready to disrupt your comfort zone and step into the identity required to build wealth. Here's how:

STEP 1 — Ask AI to identify your expansion edge.

Copy the prompt into AI and add: **"Answer this by revealing the next-level version of me I'm resisting stepping into."**

This will show you the exact point where growth wants to happen.

STEP 2 — Ask AI how your future self would respond.

Follow up with: **"Now respond as the most confident, successful version of me. What would _she_ do?"**

This shifts you into her identity immediately.

STEP 3 — Turn the insight into a choice.

Confidence is built through action, not information.

After AI answers, ask yourself:
- _What am I willing to do differently today?_
- _What boundary am I finally ready to set?_
- _What decision aligns with my future self?_

Write it down.
Do it today. No delay, no overthinking.

This is how women rise.

Confidence is not loud.
It's consistent.
And expansion is simply the art of choosing yourself.

Ask AI:

1. "What strengths am I radically underestimating?"

2. "What would be possible if I acted like a woman who wins?"

3. "What have I outgrown but haven't admitted yet?"

4. "Where do I self-abandon financially?"

5. "What do I avoid because I'm afraid of my own potential?"

6. "What is the most powerful decision I can make this month?"

7. "What am I scared will happen if I actually succeed?"

8. "What am I scared will happen if I don't?"

9. "What would I do if I trusted myself completely?"

10. "What desires am I shrinking?"

11. "What goals feel 'too big' because they're actually aligned?"

12. "What excuses am I finally ready to stop rehearsing?"

13. "Why am I safer succeeding than failing?"

14. "Why is ease more effective than struggle?"

15. "What small shift would give me instant momentum?"

SHADOW WORK FOR WEALTH

Your shadow is the part of you that:
- fears being seen
- fears being judged
- fears being resented
- fears outgrowing people
- fears being "too much"
- fears being irresponsible
- fears becoming "the wealthy one"

If you don't integrate your shadow, it will sabotage every opportunity. **Reflection:**

What do I fear becoming if I get rich?

_____
_____
_____
_____

Who do I fear disappointing?

_____
_____
_____
_____

What identity am I afraid of losing?

_____
_____
_____
_____

Where does struggle feel safer than success?

_____
_____
_____
_____

What part of wealth feels threatening?

_____
_____
_____
_____

SHADOW WORK PROMPTS

How to Use the Shadow Work Prompts

Shadow work is where real transformation happens, not through "positive thinking," but through honesty.

Your shadow is not the broken part of you.
It's the **unintegrated** part of you:
- the parts you were taught to hide
- the fears you never voiced
- the shame you absorbed
- the versions of you you left behind
- the instincts you suppressed to stay acceptable
- the power you buried because it felt dangerous
- the desires you didn't feel "allowed" to want

Money, success, and expansion trigger the shadow more than anything else. That's why you can do all the journaling, manifesting, and strategy in the world and still sabotage. These prompts help you bring your shadow *into the light* without judgment.

Here's how to use them properly:

STEP 1 — Ask AI to reveal what you're afraid to see.

Copy the prompt into AI and add: **"Answer this as if you're revealing the unconscious fear, story, or identity I've been avoiding."**

Let AI name it. Truth is grounding not scary.

STEP 2 — Notice your emotional reaction.

Before writing anything, ask yourself:
- *Where do I feel this in my body?*
- *Does this truth feel old or recent?*
- *Who taught me to fear this part of myself?*
- *What emotion is underneath the instinct to hide?*

Your reaction is the roadmap.

STEP 3 — Ask AI how to integrate this shadow.

Follow up with: **"Now answer as my highest self. How do I integrate this shadow into power instead of fear?"**

Integration turns pain into clarity. Shadow into strength. Fear into fuel.

STEP 4 — Choose one small action that reflects the integration.

Shadow work is useless without a shift.

Ask:

- *What is one thing I can do today that my old self avoided?*
- *What is one boundary I can set?*
- *What is one truth I can honor?*

Identity changes through aligned action.

Your shadow isn't your enemy, it's the part of you that's been waiting to be seen, understood, and empowered.

This is where your wealth becomes inevitable.

Ask AI:

1. "Where do I punish myself financially?"

2. "Where do I recreate familiar pain instead of unfamiliar success?"

3. "What part of me doesn't want responsibility?"

4. "What part of me wants to stay small?"

5. "What version of me is terrified of becoming wealthy?"

6. "What belief am I scared of letting go?"

7. "What emotional payoff do I get from scarcity?"

8. "What truth about myself am I resisting?"

9. "What am I finally ready to outgrow?"

10. "What shadow trait actually holds my power?"

WEALTH IDENTITY STATEMENT WORKSHEET

The Wealthy Woman I'm Becoming:
(Describe her behaviors, energy, decisions.)

_____
_____
_____
_____

The Beliefs She Holds:
(Truths you are adopting.)

_____
_____
_____
_____

The Habits She Lives By:
(Daily actions you'll integrate.)

_____
_____
_____
_____

The Identity I'm Retiring:
(Old patterns, fears, and roles you're done performing.)

_____
_____
_____
_____

My Wealth Identity Statement:
(Write one powerful paragraph. Start with: _"I am a woman who…"_)

_____
_____
_____
_____
_____

YOUR NEXT WEALTHY MOVES (ACTION PAGE)

Choose your next 3 wealth-aligned actions:

1. _____

2. _____

3. _____

Then ask AI:

"What is the most powerful way to execute each action?"

This is where mindset becomes movement.

CLOSING NOTE

You've just completed the foundation of your empire not by learning strategies, but by becoming the kind of woman who actually uses them.

Step 1 rewired the part of you that doubted, hesitated, or played small.

Now you're ready for Step 2: discovering the purpose, talent, and direction that will anchor everything you build from here.

This is where your empire stops being a dream and starts becoming a blueprint.

You're ready.

STEP 2: PURPOSE & PASSION DISCOVERY PROMPTS

"Prompts to Discover Your Purpose, Skills & Marketable Talents"

Every empire is built on purpose, not hustle.

Before strategy, before branding, before the business model, there is **clarity**:
What you're meant for.
What energizes you.
What you naturally excel at.
What people seek you out for.
What your life has been secretly preparing you to do.

Most women don't lack talent, they lack perspective. You are too close to your own genius to recognize it. This workbook helps you extract the patterns, gifts, passions, and profit pathways hidden inside your story. AI becomes your mirror, your decoder, and your clarity strategist. This is where you discover the seeds of your empire.

HOW TO USE THIS STEP

Every prompt in this workbook is designed to uncover something specific about:

- your purpose
- your skills
- your passions
- your energy
- your alignment
- your most profitable direction

To use each prompt:

1. **Copy it into AI.**
2. **Add this instruction:** "Answer this as if you're helping me clarify my purpose, strengths, and most aligned business direction."
3. **Read slowly.**
4. **Journal your reaction underneath.**
5. **Highlight anything that feels true, exciting, or confronting.**

This is where clarity begins.

PURPOSE ACTIVATION PAGE

Close your eyes and imagine this:

You wake up knowing exactly what you're meant to do.
Your work energizes you.
Your skills flow naturally.
Your passion becomes your income.
Your life aligns around who you *really* are.

Purpose isn't discovered, it's *activated*. Write what "aligned purpose" feels like to you:

When I am aligned with my purpose, I feel:

PURPOSE DISCOVERY PROMPTS

HOW TO USE THESE PROMPTS

Purpose shows up in patterns. Ask AI to reveal the patterns you've been living without noticing. Purpose discovery prompts are designed to do two things:

1. Reveal what you're meant for.

(You ask AI as if it's reading the deeper patterns, gifts, and direction in your life.)

2. Reveal what you've been ignoring.

(You reflect after and see the desires, strengths, and truths you've been too close to recognize.)

This two-step process helps you uncover the work that aligns with your soul **and** the clarity you need to choose your direction with confidence.

HOW TO USE THEM:

1. Copy the prompt and ask AI to answer "as if you're helping me uncover my purpose, gifts, and most aligned direction." Let AI reflect your patterns back to you.

2. Read the response slowly. Notice what feels true, surprising, or quietly powerful.

3. Write your own reflection underneath. This is where purpose becomes personal and meaningful.

4. Highlight the words or themes that repeat. Purpose shows up in patterns, not random guesses.

5. Let one insight guide your next aligned step. Purpose becomes clearer through action, not overthinking.

Purpose isn't something you find by chance. It's something you **recognize** through truth, clarity, and emotional resonance. Let your deeper self lead the way.

1. "What themes repeat in my life story, and what purpose do they point to?"

   _____

   _____

2. "What impact am I naturally built to create?"

   _____

   _____

3. "What have I always cared about, even before I knew why?"

   _____

   _____

4. "What desires keep resurfacing no matter how many times I ignore them?"

   _____

   _____

5. "What type of work would feel meaningful to me long-term?"

   _____

   _____

6. "What emotional or intuitive gifts shape my purpose?"

   _____

   _____

7. "In what ways has my life been preparing me for my next chapter?"

   _____

   _____

8. "What calling have I been avoiding because it feels too big?"

   _____

   _____

9. "What would I devote myself to if success were guaranteed?"

   _____

   _____

10. "What purpose becomes obvious when you look at my strengths, patterns, and personality?"

   _____

   _____

TEACHING PAGE: THE TRUTH ABOUT PURPOSE

Every woman carries a purpose she didn't consciously choose.

It forms quietly over years through the experiences that shaped you, the roles you were forced into, the gifts you discovered by accident, the passions you suppressed, and the moments that cracked you open.

Your subconscious purpose blueprint is shaped by:
- what you were praised for
- what you were criticized for
- what you had to become to survive
- what felt safe to want
- what felt dangerous to want
- what you naturally excelled at
- what you hid to fit in
- what lit you up before life got heavy
- what the world expected you to be
- what you secretly knew you could be

Purpose is not a single calling.
It's the sum of your patterns.

It determines:
- what kind of work feels meaningful
- what drains you instantly
- what energizes you without effort
- what you're naturally talented at
- what problems you're built to solve
- what direction keeps resurfacing
- what dreams refuse to die
- what identity feels the most like "you"

You are not uncovering a random passion,
you are decoding a lifetime of clues.

You're recognizing the part of you that has been there since the beginning:

the part that knows exactly where you're supposed to go next.

This page begins that recognition.

SUBCONSCIOUS DESIRE & PATTERN PROMPTS

HOW TO USE THESE PROMPTS

Your deepest desires and direction were shaped long before you ever tried to "figure out" your purpose. They live inside your subconscious, in the patterns you repeat, the roles you slip into, the dreams you abandoned, and the longings you've been taught to silence. These prompts reveal what you *actually* want, not what you were conditioned to want. To get the clearest truth, use this 3-step method:

STEP 1 — Ask AI to reveal the hidden desire or pattern.
Copy the prompt and ask: **"Answer this as if you're analyzing the subconscious desires, patterns, and deeper direction that have been shaping my life."**

AI will surface the wants, needs, and impulses you've ignored, minimized, or mislabeled as "irrational." This is where clarity begins.

STEP 2 — Let the insight land in your body, not just your mind.
Read slowly. Notice what feels:
- true
- surprising
- activating
- uncomfortable
- relieving
- familiar
- undeniable

Your subconscious responds to recognition, not logic. This is where you'll feel the difference between what you *think* you want and what you *actually* want. Awareness alone begins the recalibration.

STEP 3 — Reflect and name the truth you've avoided.
After AI mirrors the pattern back to you, journal:
- *What part of this desire have I been afraid to admit?*
- *Where in my life has this pattern already shown up?*
- *What would change if I honored this truth?*
- *What is one small aligned action I can take today?*

You are not uncovering random preferences, you are recognizing the blueprint of your purpose. These prompts help you excavate the real you beneath expectations, pressure, and noise...
so you can finally choose a future built on truth instead of conditioning.

1. "What desires have I been suppressing to stay 'practical'?"
2. "What type of work do I crave even if it scares me?"
3. "What am I drawn to again and again?"
4. "Where do I abandon myself in career decisions?"
5. "What patterns in my life reveal what I'm meant to pursue?"
6. "What environments or roles make me feel alive?"
7. "What parts of myself am I hiding that belong in my purpose?"
8. "What future am I afraid to admit I want?"
9. "What dream never really died?"
10. "What truth about myself have I been avoiding?"

WORKSHEET: PURPOSE RECOGNITION

Clarity doesn't come all at once. It arrives in patterns, themes, repeated truths, and subtle moments of recognition.

This worksheet helps you *catch* the clarity that has been rising through every prompt, every insight, and every reflection.

Use this page to:
- gather the threads
- capture the patterns
- name what you actually want
- articulate the purpose that's been trying to reveal itself

Don't try to "get it perfect."
Purpose is a living thing. It sharpens as you act.

Let these lines become the first spoken version of the woman you're becoming.

Write freely.
Write honestly.
Write what feels true in your body, not just your mind.

This is where your purpose takes form.

The patterns I keep seeing in my answers:

_____

_____

What I now know I actually want:

_____

_____

Purpose sentences that feel true:

_____

_____

TEACHING PAGE: THE SKILLS YOU IGNORE

You underestimate yourself because your gifts feel "normal" to you. But what feels normal to you is often extraordinary to others. Your real strengths come from life, not job titles. Most women don't lack talent, they lack *recognition*.

You underestimate yourself because your gifts feel "normal" to you. But the things that feel effortless, obvious, or second nature to you are often the very things other people find extraordinary. Your real strengths aren't defined by job titles, certifications, or corporate approval. They're shaped by:

- the roles you've had to play
- the challenges you survived
- the responsibilities you carried too young
- the patterns you repeat naturally
- the emotional intelligence you developed without trying
- the instincts you trust without explanation
- the creativity you use to solve everyday problems
- the leadership you show without thinking
- the resilience life forced you to build

Your most valuable skills are often hiding in plain sight disguised as "just who I am."

Skills like:

- making people feel understood
- organizing chaos
- seeing the bigger picture
- staying calm when others spiral
- communicating clearly
- intuitively reading a room
- turning ideas into action
- making others feel safe
- creating beauty or order
- solving problems quickly
- noticing details others overlook

These aren't accidents. They're indicators of your purpose.

When you dismiss your own strengths, you disconnect from the impact you're meant to have. When you finally *name* them, everything begins to click: your direction, your confidence, your opportunities, your path forward.

This page begins the part of your journey where you finally see yourself clearly not through modesty or habit, but through **truth**.

Your skills aren't small. You've just never been taught to honor them.

SKILL & TALENT PROMPTS

HOW TO USE THESE PROMPTS

Your greatest strengths rarely feel like strengths at all
they feel like "just who I am."

These prompts help you uncover the talents you've minimized, dismissed, or never recognized as valuable. To get the clearest reflection of your true abilities, use this 3-step method:

STEP 1 — Ask AI to reveal the skills you've been downplaying.

Copy the prompt into AI and add: **"Answer this as if you're analyzing the natural strengths, life-built skills, and talents I underestimate or overlook."**

AI will highlight the abilities you've normalized. The ones that feel effortless to you but extraordinary to others. This is where recognition begins.

STEP 2 — Let the insight challenge your self-perception.

Read slowly and notice what feels:
- unexpectedly accurate
- validating
- uncomfortable
- surprising
- empowering
- obvious in hindsight

You are learning to see yourself the way the world already sees you. Awareness is the first step toward confidence.

STEP 3 — Claim the strengths that belong to you.

After AI reflects your skills back to you, journal:
- *Which of these strengths have I minimized?*
- *Where have these skills already shaped my life?*
- *What opportunities could these strengths create for me?*
- *What am I finally ready to own about who I am?*

These prompts help you name and claim the abilities that form the backbone of your purpose and the foundation of your empire.

You are not discovering new strengths,
you are finally acknowledging the ones you've carried all along.

"What are my natural strengths that I overlook?"

_____

_____

"What skills have I gained from difficult experiences?"

_____

_____

"What am I better at than most people?"

_____

_____

"What do people consistently seek my help with?"

_____

_____

"Which of my qualities are actually marketable skills?"

_____

_____

"What have I mastered without realizing it?"

_____

_____

"What strengths do I minimize because they come easily?"

_____

_____

"What emotional or intuitive skills do I carry?"

_____

_____

"What traits make me a natural leader, creator, or teacher?"

_____

_____

"What abilities would surprise me if someone praised them?"

_____

_____

TEACHING PAGE:
PASSION & ENERGY ARE NOT THE SAME

Most women confuse passion with alignment.

A passion is something you *like.*
Energy is something that *sustains you.*
And your purpose must be built on energy not entertainment.

Passion can excite you, but energy reveals the truth:
- Passion is what feels fun.
- Energy is what feels natural.
- Passion is what you daydream about.
- Energy is what you effortlessly slip into.
- Passion lights you up for a moment.
- Energy fuels you over the long haul.

You can be passionate about something that drains you.
You can feel indifferent toward something that was actually meant for you.
You can love a hobby but hate doing it for money.
You can feel alive doing something the world doesn't consider "a passion."
Your energy holds the map, not your imagination. Your life has shown you where your energy goes:
- What creates momentum instead of pressure
- What activities make time disappear
- What roles fit your nervous system
- What responsibilities feel lighter than expected
- What contributions feel like oxygen instead of obligation
- What types of work leave you fuller, not emptier
- What desires return even after you ignore them

Energy is honest. Energy is consistent. Energy doesn't perform, it reveals.

Your long-term purpose lives in the intersection of: **what you enjoy + what energizes you + what sustains you.**

This page bridges the gap between excitement and alignment, between what looks appealing and what actually nourishes your spirit.

When you learn to follow your energy, clarity becomes inevitable. It stops feeling like searching… and starts feeling like remembering.

PASSION & ENERGY PROMPTS

HOW TO USE THESE PROMPTS

Passion excites you, but energy sustains you.

These prompts help you identify the work, roles, and creative lanes that *fuel* you rather than drain you, so you can build an aligned business that lasts. To uncover the truth of where your energy naturally flows, use this 3-step method:

STEP 1 — Ask AI to analyze your energetic patterns.

Copy the prompt into AI and add: **"Answer this as if you're revealing what activities, environments, and roles energize me and which ones drain me."**

AI will highlight the patterns you haven't consciously recognized, the places where your energy rises or disappears. This is where alignment starts.

STEP 2 — Let the insight land in your body.

Read slowly and notice what feels:
- accurate
- relieving
- validating
- surprising
- energizing
- heavy
- undeniable

Your body always tells the truth. Energy is honest, even when your mind isn't. Awareness of your energetic patterns prevents burnout and leads you toward a purpose that actually fits.

STEP 3 — Identify the work that feels sustainable for you.

After AI reflects your energy patterns, journal:
- *Where does my energy naturally rise?*
- *What drains me even if I'm good at it?*
- *What tasks or roles feel like home?*
- *What type of work could I sustain for years?*
- *What is one aligned action I can take today?*

These prompts help you uncover the work you are built for, the work that nourishes your spirit, matches your nervous system, and lights up your long-term purpose. This is where excitement meets sustainability.

"What activities give me energy rather than drain it?"

"What could I talk about for hours?"

"What do I research or obsess over naturally?"

"What parts of my personality feel most alive?"

"What roles or tasks feel like a match for my energy?"

"What used to excite me before responsibilities weighed me down?"

"What hobbies or interests point toward my purpose?"

"What type of work feels natural instead of forced?"

"What creative outlets have I abandoned that I should revisit?"

"What excites me even when no one supports it?"

DAILY CLARITY ROUTINE

A 10-Minute Ritual to Build Self-Awareness, Direction & Momentum

Purpose is not found in one breakthrough moment. Purpose is built slowly, consistently, and intentionally.

This 10-minute clarity routine helps you align your inner world before you build your outer empire. When you practice it daily, you begin to recognize patterns, desires, strengths, and truths you used to overlook. Clarity doesn't arrive all at once, it *compounds*. Here's your simple, powerful daily ritual:

1. Ask One Purpose Prompt

Begin with a question that pulls you into truth and self-recognition.
Purpose lives in your desires, instincts, and lived experience.
This prompt sets the tone by reconnecting you to what matters.

2. Ask One Skill Prompt

Next, bring forward the strengths you underestimate.
Every day, a different talent or ability will reveal itself.
Over time, you'll begin seeing the architecture of your purpose.

3. Ask One Energy Prompt

Now ask AI what fuels you, not just what excites you. Your energy patterns determine what's sustainable and sustainability is the backbone of your future business.

4. Journal 3 Insights

Write down the three things that stand out the most.
They could be truths, surprises, discomforts, or confirmations.
These insights become your compass, your inner roadmap.

5. Choose One Aligned Action

Clarity is useless without movement.
Choose one simple action that matches what you learned today: a message, a task, a boundary, a brainstorm, a small shift. The goal is not perfection, it's direction.

When you act in alignment daily, momentum becomes inevitable.

Why This Works

This ritual rewires your brain to operate from truth instead of confusion, comparison, or overwhelm.

Every day, your vision sharpens.
Every day, your confidence grows.
Every day, you take one more step toward the woman you're becoming.

Clarity isn't an event. It's a practice, and she compounds beautifully.

MONETIZATION PROMPTS

Monetization is not about forcing yourself into a business model. It's about recognizing where your gifts, energy, and value intersect with what people are willing to pay for. These prompts help you translate your strengths into offers, niches, and income pathways that feel natural, not overwhelming. Use the 3-step method below for the clearest, most aligned answers:

STEP 1 — Ask AI to connect your gifts with profitable opportunities.

Copy each prompt into AI and add: **"Answer this as if you're identifying my most monetizable skills, strengths, and opportunities based on who I actually am, not who I'm trying to be."**

AI will reveal where your earning potential already exists. You'll see the skills you've overlooked, the paths that feel easy for you, and the niches where your abilities stand out. This is where monetization starts to make sense.

STEP 2 — Let the answers expand your perspective.

Read slowly and notice what feels:
- exciting
- doable
- obvious once you see it
- aligned with your energy
- like, "Wait… I could actually sell this"
- grounded instead of stressful
- surprisingly clear

Your subconscious already knows where your money is. These prompts help you recognize it consciously.

STEP 3 — Turn insight into your first (or next) offer.

After AI reveals your monetizable gifts, journal:
- *What could I create quickly?*
- *What feels fun instead of heavy?*
- *Who could I help right now?*
- *What problem do I naturally solve?*
- *What offer feels like the easiest win?*

Then choose ONE idea to act on this week. Monetization works best when you start simple: one offer, one audience, one transformation. You don't find your business, you build it from the gifts you already carry.

"What would people realistically pay me for?"

_____

_____

"Based on my strengths, what digital products could I create?"

_____

_____

"What transformation could I help someone achieve?"

_____

_____

"What problems am I uniquely equipped to solve?"

_____

_____

"What skills of mine are monetizable right now?"

_____

_____

"What would be my easiest first offer?"

_____

_____

"What businesses align with my energy and talents?"

_____

_____

"Who is already making money doing something similar?"

_____

_____

"What niche could I dominate quickly?"

_____

_____

"What high-value offer could I create from my skill set?"

_____

_____

TEACHING PAGE:
SHADOW WORK FOR CLARITY

Most people think they're confused. They're not. They're scared.

Confusion is often a disguise your mind uses to protect you from the truth you're not ready to claim. Shadow work helps you separate real confusion from emotional camouflage.

Fear is subtle. It doesn't shout. it whispers. It shows up as:

- procrastination
- "I don't know where to start"
- overthinking
- staying busy instead of aligned
- waiting for a sign
- second-guessing your desires
- doubting your capability
- convincing yourself you need more clarity before you move

But underneath almost every "I'm confused" moment is a deeper fear:

- Fear of failure — *What if I try and it doesn't work?*
- Fear of visibility — *What if people judge me?*
- Fear of success — *What if I can't handle it?*
- Fear of choosing wrong — *What if I mess up my life?*
- Fear of being seen — *What if they see the real me?*
- Fear of desire — *What if I want too much?*

Your shadow isn't the dark part of you, it's the part of you that learned to hide to stay safe. Shadow work clears the fog by revealing:

- the fear underneath the hesitation
- the truth underneath the confusion
- the desire underneath the doubt
- the pattern underneath the self-sabotage
- the identity underneath the insecurity

You don't do shadow work to shame yourself. You do it to *understand* yourself.

When you bring light to the part of you that's afraid, clarity stops feeling like a mystery and starts feeling like relief.

Your shadow isn't your enemy. It's your compass.

It shows you exactly where you're meant to grow next.

SHADOW WORK PROMPTS

HOW TO USE THESE PROMPTS

Shadow work isn't about digging for darkness, it's about revealing the fear beneath your confusion so you can finally see clearly.

These prompts help you uncover the emotional patterns, protective mechanisms, and hidden beliefs blocking your purpose. Use the 3-step method below for the deepest clarity:

STEP 1 — Ask AI to reveal the fears blocking your clarity.

Copy the prompt into AI and add: **"Answer this as if you're uncovering the fears, beliefs, and emotional patterns that are preventing me from seeing or claiming my purpose."**

AI will surface what your subconscious has been protecting you from: the fear, the avoidance, the identity you've outgrown, the story you're still living inside. This is where the fog begins to lift.

STEP 2 — Let the truth settle before you respond.

Read slowly and notice what feels:
- uncomfortable
- too accurate
- strangely familiar
- relieving
- triggering
- clarifying
- like something you've always known but never said

Shadow work doesn't hurt, it *reveals*. And recognition is the beginning of freedom.

STEP 3 — Rewrite the story from a place of honesty.

After AI exposes the fear or block, journal:
- *What part of this feels true?*
- *Where have I lived this pattern?*
- *What emotion have I been avoiding?*
- *What belief am I finally ready to release?*
- *What new story am I choosing instead?*
- *What aligned action matches the new story?*

Shadow work isn't about fixing yourself. It's about seeing yourself clearly and choosing not to abandon the woman you're becoming.

This is clarity that lasts.

"What am I afraid will happen if I choose the wrong path?"

"What part of me fears being seen in my purpose?"

"Where do I sabotage clarity because clarity requires action?"

"What belief is keeping me small?"

"What identity am I afraid to step out of?"

"What success am I scared to admit I want?"

"What negative story about myself needs to be rewritten?"

"What am I protecting by staying confused?"

PURPOSE STATEMENT WORKSHEET

A space to name the truth you've been circling.

Your purpose isn't a sentence you invent, it's a sentence you *remember.*

Use this page to translate everything you've discovered
into a clear, grounded, embodied statement of who you are and what you're here to do.

Take your time.
Breathe.
Let the truth come through.

My Purpose (First Draft):

Let it be messy, intuitive, imperfect. Write what feels close to true.

_____

_____

_____

Refined Purpose Statement:

Now shape it. Make it clearer, simpler, and more aligned with your gifts, energy, and desires.

_____

_____

_____

Purpose That Feels True in My Body:

This is the most important one.
Write the version that gives you goosebumps, a soft exhale, or a quiet sense of "oh... that's me."

_____

_____

_____

MY FIRST 3 BUSINESS DIRECTIONS

Your purpose becomes real the moment it becomes directional.

You don't need the full business built yet. You just need **your first three aligned directions**, the pathways that feel possible, energizing, and true based on everything you've uncovered in Step 2.

These aren't commitments. They're starting points.

Choose the three directions that feel:
- aligned with your purpose
- supported by your skills
- fueled by your energy
- exciting to imagine
- sustainable long-term
- true in your body, not just on paper

Let this be intuitive.

Direction 1:

The first idea that feels the most aligned right now.

_____

_____

_____

Direction 2:

An idea that feels energizing or creatively exciting.

_____

_____

_____

Direction 3:

An idea that feels surprisingly possible or naturally "you."

_____

_____

_____

CLOSING NOTE

You are no longer wandering in circles.
You are no longer waiting for inspiration to strike.
You are no longer trying to "figure it out."
You are choosing.

You are stepping into clarity, alignment, and direction, not in theory, but in truth.

This chapter marks the moment you stop searching for your purpose and start building **from** it.

Every prompt you answered,
every insight that surfaced,
every fear you confronted,
it all brought you closer to the woman you're becoming.

You are not behind.
You are not late.
You are not confused.
You are ready.

Your empire begins here with this clarity, this honesty, this self-recognition.

And in **Step 3**, we turn this inner knowing into outer structure.
We build your first offers.
Your business blueprint.
Your income pathways.
Your direction with momentum.

Step 2 revealed who you are.
Step 3 builds what you're meant to create.

Turn the page, my love.
Your empire awaits.

STEP 3:
THE MILLION-DOLLAR IDEAS GENERATOR

"Prompts to Ask AI for 100+ Business Ideas Based on Your Personality, Lifestyle, Strengths

Now that you know who you are…
it's time to discover what you can *build*.

Step 3 is where your purpose becomes practical. Where your clarity becomes creative. Where your identity becomes opportunity. Most women think ideas magically appear. They don't. Ideas are generated deliberately, strategically, and in alignment with:

- your personality
- your skills
- your energy
- your desires
- your income goals
- your lifestyle
- your values
- your strengths
- your nervous system
- your purpose

Your business is not something you guess. It's something you *design*. Step 3 turns AI into your business architect, the strategist who hands you a list of ideas that make sense for who you are, what you want, and how you operate. This is the step where women stop picking random business models and start choosing the ones aligned with their actual lives. Welcome to the idea generator that changes everything.

HOW TO USE THIS STEP

Every prompt in this step is designed to create:
- aligned business ideas
- profitable business ideas
- sustainable business ideas
- ideas shaped by who you actually are

Not generic suggestions. Not "what everyone else is doing." Not someone else's blueprint.

To get the best results:

1. **Copy the prompt into AI.**
2. **Add this instruction:**
   "Answer this as if you're designing profitable business ideas based on my personality, strengths, lifestyle, and income goals."
3. **Let AI generate options.**
4. **Highlight ideas that feel like a YES.**
5. **Discard anything that feels heavy, forced, or unaligned.**
6. **Circle the ideas that feel both exciting and sustainable.**

You are not choosing your business yet. You are generating possibilities. This is where your empire begins to take shape.

TEACHING PAGE:
THE TRUTH ABOUT BUSINESS IDEAS

Most women don't lack ideas, they lack *aligned* ideas. Ideas that actually fit their:

- Energy
- Skills
- Personality
- Schedule
- income goals
- creative style
- nervous system
- lived experience
- zones of genius

You can build any business. But not every business is built for *you*. The right idea will feel like:

- relief
- alignment
- excitement
- clarity
- "this makes sense"
- "this feels like me"
- "this is doable"

The wrong idea will feel like:

- Pressure
- Overwhelm
- Confusion
- Avoidance
- instant exhaustion
- "I should do this"
- "I guess I could try"

The right idea fits seamlessly into your life. The wrong idea requires you to abandon yourself to maintain it. Aligned ideas always come from three places:

1. **Your strengths**
2. **Your energy patterns**
3. **Your lived experience**

This step helps AI combine all three. And when you see the ideas matched to your essence, everything begins to click.

THE MILLION-DOLLAR IDEA PROMPTS

These are the foundational prompts designed to generate **dozens even hundreds of business ideas** that fit *your* personality, *your* strengths, and *your* path to wealth. These prompts are not random. They are strategic, layered, and intentionally crafted to help AI map out:

- your most profitable business directions
- your fastest path to income
- your deepest aligned work
- your sustainable long-term models
- your premium pivots
- your scalable brand possibilities

Each section is structured to mirror the clarity process in Step 2 meaning:

You will uncover the ideas that feel true in your body, not just smart on paper.

Each category below includes:

1. **How to use the prompt** (so AI responds with depth instead of surface-level ideas)
2. **The 3-step integration method** (based on Step 2's somatic clarity style)
3. **The actual prompts**

These are your million-dollar generators.

HOW TO USE THESE PROMPTS

Every business idea becomes ten times clearer when you ask AI to analyze: **who you are + how you operate + what energizes you + what you want financially.**

Before you enter any prompt, add this line: **"Answer as if you're generating profitable, aligned business ideas based on my personality, strengths, lifestyle, energy, and income goals."**

This ensures you get **quality** ideas, the kind that make you think: *This is literally perfect for me.*

THE 3-STEP MILLION-DOLLAR IDEA METHOD

Pulling directly from the Step 2 clarity style but evolved for ideation:

STEP 1 — Ask the prompt.

Let AI generate dozens of directions. Do not judge yet.

STEP 2 — Circle the ideas that feel like:

- Relief
- Recognition
- Alignment
- "Oh, fuck, that's me"
- "I could actually do that right now"

These are the emotional green lights.

STEP 3 — Cross out anything that feels like:

- Pressure
- Forcing
- Performing
- a version of you you're leaving behind
- busywork
- Stress disguised as opportunity

These are your red lights. You are not choosing a business yet, you're **choosing resonance**.

SECTION 1
PERSONALITY-BASED BUSINESS IDEAS

HOW TO USE THESE PROMPTS

Your personality holds the blueprint for how you're meant to create, lead, serve, and earn. Your natural tendencies reveal which business models will thrive under your care. To uncover your personality-based business lanes, use this 3-step method:

STEP 1 — Ask AI to analyze your personality as a business foundation.

Add this instruction: *"Answer this as if you're generating business ideas that perfectly fit my personality, strengths, and preferences."*

STEP 2 — Notice what feels like you.

Circle ideas that feel:
- Effortless
- True
- Exciting
- Comfortable
- Obvious
- Aligned

STEP 3 — Keep only what feels sustainable.

If you can see yourself doing it for 3+ years, it stays. If it feels like an identity you'd have to force yourself into, it goes.

1. "Generate business ideas based on my personality type and the way I naturally operate."
2. "What business models match my strengths, temperament, and core traits?"
3. "If my personality became a profitable brand, what would it look like?"
4. "What roles and business types fit how I think, communicate, and create?"
5. "What business ideas align with my natural leadership and creative style?"
6. "Based on my personality, what would be my easiest path to $10K/month?"

7. "What types of businesses would allow me to stay authentic instead of performative?"
8. "What business ideas feel like an extension of who I am?"
9. "What would I build if my business model matched my personality perfectly?"
10. "What are 20 business ideas that align with my personality strengths and nervous system?"

SECTION 2
SKILL-BASED BUSINESS IDEAS

HOW TO USE THESE PROMPTS

Your skills, especially the ones you undervalue are the foundation of your most profitable ideas. To uncover your skill-based business lanes:

STEP 1 — Ask AI to identify monetizable skills.

Add: *"Answer as if you're generating business ideas based on my strongest skills and talents."*

STEP 2 — Notice the ideas that feel natural.

STEP 3 — Choose the ideas that feel scalable.

1. "What business ideas could I build from my natural skills?"
2. "What have I mastered that could become a business?"
3. "What skills of mine are the most profitable?"
4. "What business models align with my overlooked strengths?"
5. "What businesses could I build based on the challenges I've overcome?"
6. "What businesses align with my ability to lead, teach, or create?"
7. "What business ideas would allow me to monetize the strengths I use daily?"
8. "What are 20 digital product ideas based on my skills?"
9. "What service-based businesses could I launch with the talents I already have?"
10. "What business ideas fit my natural gifts and life-built abilities?"

SECTION 3
ENERGY-BASED BUSINESS IDEAS

HOW TO USE THESE PROMPTS

Energy is the real predictor of long-term success. A business you hate drains you. A business aligned with your energy fuels you. To uncover energy-aligned business ideas:

STEP 1 — Ask AI to map your energetic patterns.

Add: *"Answer as if you're identifying business ideas based on what energizes me and what drains me."*

STEP 2 — Notice what feels light, exciting, and sustainable.

STEP 3 — Reject anything heavy or forced.

1. "What business ideas match my energy patterns and the type of work that fuels me?"
2. "What business models would be sustainable for me long-term?"
3. "What type of business could I run without burning out?"
4. "What work feels like a natural fit for my energy?"
5. "What businesses align with how my nervous system operates?"
6. "What entrepreneurial roles would feel like home to me?"
7. "What ideas would I still enjoy 5 years from now?"
8. "What business ideas give me momentum instead of pressure?"
9. "Generate 25 business ideas based solely on what energizes me."
10. "What business models are aligned with how I naturally move through the world?"

SECTION 4
INCOME GOAL–BASED BUSINESS IDEAS

HOW TO USE THESE PROMPTS

You don't build a $1M business using strategies meant for $50K businesses. To generate financially aligned ideas:

STEP 1 — Tell AI your income goal.

Examples:
$5K/month
$10K/month
$30K/month
$100K/month
$1M/year

STEP 2 — Ask AI to align ideas with those numbers.

STEP 3 — Keep the ones that feel both profitable and possible.

1. "What business ideas match my first income goal of $____ per month?"
2. "What business could realistically get me to $10K/month the fastest?"
3. "What business ideas have a clear path to $30K/month?"
4. "What business models scale to $100K/month or $1M/year?"
5. "What ideas fit my income goals, energy, and skill set?"
6. "What business would give me the biggest ROI with the least resistance?"
7. "What are my million-dollar pathways based on who I am?"
8. "What business ideas could create passive or semi-passive income for me?"
9. "What are 20 high-income business ideas aligned with my personality?"
10. "If my goal is $1M+ per year, what idea makes the most sense for me?"

SECTION 5
LIFESTYLE-BASED BUSINESS IDEAS

HOW TO USE THESE PROMPTS

Your lifestyle determines the structure your business must fit into. To generate ideas aligned with your real life:

STEP 1 — Ask AI to factor in your lifestyle, schedule, and responsibilities.

STEP 2 — Choose the ideas that support how you actually want to live.

STEP 3 — Notice anything that would require sacrifice you don't want to make.

1. "What business ideas fit the lifestyle I want to live?"
2. "Generate business ideas that align with my time, energy, and routine."
3. "What business models match the flexibility I need?"
4. "What businesses can I run without constant pressure or deadlines?"
5. "What business would give me freedom, not burnout?"
6. "What ideas fit the life I have now and the life I want next?"
7. "What business ideas allow me to work from anywhere?"
8. "What are 20 low-stress business ideas that match my lifestyle?"
9. "What business aligns with the way I want my days to feel?"
10. "If I designed a business around the life I desire, what ideas emerge?"

SECTION 6
PURPOSE-ALIGNED BUSINESS IDEAS

HOW TO USE THESE PROMPTS

This is where Step 2 comes alive. You have a purpose blueprint now, let's turn it into business models.

STEP 1 — Ask AI to pull from your purpose patterns.

STEP 2 — Choose the ideas that match your deeper calling.

STEP 3 — Reject anything that feels disconnected from who you're becoming.

1. "What business ideas align with my purpose blueprint?"
2. "What business would allow me to express my calling?"
3. "What ideas match my gifts, desires, and deeper direction?"
4. "What business ideas feel like destiny, not effort?"
5. "What businesses help me create the impact I'm meant to create?"
6. "What ideas reflect the woman I'm becoming?"
7. "What business could be my legacy?"
8. "What business ideas align with the patterns in Step 2?"
9. "What ideas are both purposeful and profitable?"
10. "What business would feel like a full-body yes?"

SECTION 7
ARCHETYPE-BASED BUSINESS IDEAS

"Prompts that match your creative, leadership, money & shadow archetypes to profitable business models."

HOW TO USE THESE PROMPTS

Your archetypes reveal:
- your magnetism
- your leadership style
- your shadow gifts
- your money patterns
- your creative genius
- your brand voice
- your audience resonance

When you build a business that aligns with your archetype, everything feels easier:
- content feels natural
- offers feel aligned
- selling feels ethical
- momentum feels organic

These prompts help AI read your archetype and turn it into aligned, profitable business directions.

STEP 1 — Tell AI your archetype (or have it guess).

Optional: *"Analyze my communication style so far, what archetype do I embody?"*

STEP 2 — Let AI generate ideas based on your archetype's strengths.

STEP 3 — Circle the ideas that feel like destiny.

1. "Generate 20 business ideas based on my core archetype."
2. "What business models match my creator archetype?"
3. "What business aligns with my mentor/teacher archetype?"
4. "What business fits my rebel/disruptor archetype?"
5. "If my archetype became a brand, what would I sell?"
6. "What business ideas match my shadow archetype gifts?"
7. "How does my money archetype influence my ideal business model?"
8. "What business suits my communication archetype?"
9. "What business ideas match my leadership archetype?"
10. "What business models match my intuitive/psychic archetype?"
11. "Generate ideas based on my highest self archetype."
12. "If my archetype ran an online empire, what would it include?"
13. "What digital products match my archetype's strengths?"
14. "What business would amplify my natural magnetism?"

15. "What niche fits the way my archetype solves problems?"
16. "Generate 10 premium offers based on my archetype."
17. "What business models fit both my light and shadow archetypes?"
18. "What community or membership fits my archetype?"
19. "What type of brand storytelling matches my archetype?"
20. "What business ideas would allow my archetype to build wealth effortlessly?"

SECTION 8
FAST CASH BUSINESS IDEAS

"Prompts for ideas you can launch in 7 days, 14 days, 30 days."

HOW TO USE THESE PROMPTS

Not every idea is long-term. Sometimes you need money *now*. These prompts tell AI to generate:
- quick wins
- low barrier ideas
- fast-to-market offers
- simple MVPs
- instant revenue opportunities

These are businesses you can launch *immediately*, with minimal setup, minimal cost, and maximum speed.

STEP 1 — Set your timeframe.

Examples:
7 days
14 days
30 days
90 days

STEP 2 — Ask AI to generate ONLY fast, simple, launchable ideas.

STEP 3 — Choose one to execute *this week*.

1. "Give me 25 business ideas I can launch in 7 days."
2. "What business could I start this weekend?"
3. "What digital products could I create in under 24 hours?"
4. "What service could I offer immediately with zero setup?"
5. "What could I sell today using the skills I already have?"
6. "What business ideas could bring in my first $500 fast?"
7. "What business models get me to $2K in the next 14 days?"
8. "What $27–$97 offers could I launch instantly?"
9. "What 30-day business ideas require no audience?"
10. "What can I launch quickly if I need money by next month?"
11. "Give me 20 low-tech business ideas I can start immediately."
12. "What can I create and sell within 48 hours?"

13. "What business ideas fit my need for fast revenue?"
14. "What mini-offers could I bundle and sell this week?"
15. "What services could I sell to my existing network today?"
16. "What recession-proof fast-cash ideas fit my skills?"
17. "What business could generate income before the end of the month?"
18. "What small digital programs could I pre-sell immediately?"
19. "What 1:1 offers could I launch instantly with no tech?"
20. "If I needed $5K quickly, what business ideas make the most sense?"

SECTION 9
TREND & MARKET-BASED BUSINESS IDEAS
"Prompts that use timing, trends, and current market demand."

HOW TO USE THESE PROMPTS

Money follows attention. Money follows trends. Money follows consumer behavior. When you build a business aligned with what the world is already paying for, everything becomes easier.

These prompts tell AI to analyze:
- market trends
- buyer psychology
- emerging industries
- seasonal cycles
- viral niches
- creator economy shifts
- AI opportunities
- consumer spending patterns

STEP 1 — Ask AI to analyze current trends.
STEP 2 — Choose ideas aligned with your skill set.
STEP 3 — Pick the ideas with staying power + momentum.

1. "Generate business ideas based on current market trends."
2. "What niches are exploding right now that match my skills?"
3. "What businesses will be in high demand next year?"
4. "What market gaps exist that I could fill?"
5. "What trending digital products could I create?"
6. "What niches are profitable but underserved?"
7. "What business ideas align with AI trends?"
8. "What business models are booming in the creator economy?"
9. "What evergreen trends could I build a business around?"
10. "What micro-niches could I dominate quickly?"
11. "What content niches have high growth and low competition?"
12. "What trends match my personality and energy?"

13. "What seasonal trends could I capitalize on?"
14. "What business ideas align with the holiday shopping surge?"
15. "What niches will be profitable for the next decade?"
16. "What future-of-work trends create business opportunities for me?"
17. "What social media trends could I turn into income?"
18. "What AI-assisted businesses will grow fastest?"
19. "What trending customer problems can I solve?"
20. "Give me 20 high-demand business ideas based on emerging industries."

SECTION 10
IDENTITY-BASED BUSINESS IDEAS

Prompts that ask: "What business would the highest version of me build?"

HOW TO USE THESE PROMPTS

Your identity determines your destiny. Your business must reflect the woman you're becoming not the version you're leaving behind. These prompts ask AI to generate ideas based on your:

- highest self
- healed self
- future self
- wealth identity
- CEO identity
- embodied self
- aligned self

STEP 1 — Name the identity you're stepping into.
STEP 2 — Ask AI to generate ideas from that identity.
STEP 3 — Choose the ideas that feel expansive, not overwhelming.

1. "What business would my highest self build?"
2. "What business ideas match the woman I'm becoming?"
3. "What business aligns with my wealthy identity?"
4. "What business would my confident CEO self choose?"
5. "What business ideas match my healed version?"
6. "What business ideas reflect my future lifestyle?"
7. "What businesses fit the version of me who doesn't self-abandon?"
8. "What ideas feel like a full-body yes?"
9. "What business ideas feel like destiny instead of effort?"
10. "What business would I choose if I trusted myself fully?"
11. "Generate 20 ideas that match my next-level identity."
12. "What ideas align with how my soul wants to create?"
13. "What business would I build if I wasn't scared?"

14. "What ideas match the identity I'm stepping into this year?"
15. "What business would I build if success were guaranteed?"
16. "What business matches my luxurious, elevated version?"
17. "What business mirrors my authentic self-expression?"
18. "What business aligns with my empowered feminine energy?"
19. "What business would my most confident self grow to $1M?"
20. "What ideas would I choose if I were already the woman I dream of being?"

THE 100 IDEAS MASTER PROMPT

This page is designed to be THE moment of Step 3.

A mic-drop prompt women screenshot, save, and obsess over.

Copy/paste this directly into AI:

"Generate a list of 100 personalized business ideas for me. Use my personality, strengths, lifestyle, income goals, energy patterns, purpose blueprint, lived experience, creative style, and nervous system. Include digital products, services, evergreen offers, fast-cash ideas, passive income, AI-powered ideas, niche brands, content businesses, and scalable long-term pathways. Make every idea uniquely aligned to who I am and who I'm becoming."

WORKSHEET
BUSINESS IDEAS THAT FEEL TRUE

Write the ideas that stood out. The ones that felt like recognition instead of guessing.

Ideas that feel aligned:

_____

_____

Ideas that feel energizing:

_____

_____

Ideas that feel profitable:

_____

_____

Ideas that feel like "me":

_____

_____

Ideas I want to explore deeper:

_____

_____

CLOSING NOTE

You are no longer guessing your business ideas. You are generating them: intentionally, strategically, and in alignment with who you are. You have just built the foundation of your empire:

- Clarity
- Direction
- Alignment
- Momentum
- Identity
- Purpose
- Possibility

Step 2 revealed who you are. Step 3 reveals what you can build. Step 4 will turn these ideas into your full business blueprint. Turn the page, my love. Your empire is forming.

STEP 4:
THE EMPIRE MAP

"Prompts to Build Your Custom Business Ecosystem"

A guided blueprint to design your offers, products, services, income streams, and long-term brand, all tailored to who you truly are.

Your purpose is clear. Your ideas are alive. Now it's time to **build the empire that holds them.** Step 4 is where vision becomes structure. Where possibility becomes direction. Where alignment becomes a business model. This step teaches you to use AI as your strategist, your offer architect, product designer, monetization partner, and long-term brand advisor.

Here, you learn to ask:
- What would my signature offer be?
- What digital products fit my skills and energy?
- What services match my strengths and lifestyle?
- What recurring revenue streams fit the way I work?
- What long-term brand could this grow into?
- What is the ecosystem that turns this into a business?

This is where your first aligned business takes shape not from pressure, but from truth. Your empire starts with intention. Now we give it structure.

IDENTITY ACTIVATION

Become the Woman Who Builds What Lasts This step isn't about hustling. It's about architecture. You are not building a business, you're building the foundation of your empire. You are stepping into the identity of a woman who:
- chooses with clarity
- creates with intention
- sells with ease
- leads with purpose
- scales with confidence

This is where you become a builder, not of tasks, but of legacy.

WHAT STEP 4 IS

Step 2 helped you find yourself. Step 3 helped you find your ideas. **Step 4 helps you shape your empire.** This step teaches you to use AI to map:
- your signature offer
- your product ecosystem
- your services
- your recurring revenue
- your marketing flow
- your brand identity
- your future empire

By the end of this step, you will have a clear, structured ecosystem not just ideas, but a blueprint.

HOW TO USE THIS WORKBOOK

Every prompt in Step 4 helps you design a business that fits:

- your personality
- your purpose
- your skills
- your energy
- your income goals
- your lifestyle
- your long-term vision

To use each prompt:

1. **Copy it into AI.**
2. Add: *"Answer as if you're helping me design a profitable, sustainable business ecosystem based on who I actually am."*
3. Read slowly.
4. Circle anything that feels:
   - aligned
   - exciting
   - possible
   - natural
   - clarifying
5. Cross out anything that feels:
   - draining
   - performative
   - stressful
   - overly complex
   - "old identity"
6. Build from the pieces that feel true.

This step is not about perfection. It's about architecture. It's about building a business that feels like you and grows with you. Your ecosystem begins here. This is not a business textbook. This is a design studio. To get the most out of Step 4:

1. Ask the prompt.
2. Tell AI to base answers on your personality, energy, purpose, and income goals.
3. Do not rush.
4. Circle the ideas that feel like expansion.
5. Cross out anything that feels forced.
6. Build only from what feels aligned and easeful.

This workbook is about alignment, not performance.

TEACHING PAGE:
THE TRUTH ABOUT BUILDING AN EMPIRE

Business clarity doesn't come from guessing. It comes from structure.

Your business ecosystem is shaped by:

- what you're good at
- what energizes you
- what feels natural to sell
- what fits your lifestyle
- what aligns with your income goals
- what your future self would build
- what solves a real problem for your audience
- what you could sustain long-term

Most women think they need "a niche" or "an offer."

What they actually need is a **map**, a structure that holds:

- your signature offer
- your digital products
- your services
- your passive income
- your recurring revenue
- your marketing flow
- your long-term brand identity

Your empire is built in layers:

Layer 1 — The Offer You Can Sell Right Now
(Your easiest, most aligned starting point)

Layer 2 — Digital Products That Scale
(Your passive income ecosystem)

Layer 3 — Recurring Revenue Streams
(Memberships, subscriptions, retainers)

Layer 4 — Your Signature Brand Direction
(The larger identity you're growing into)

Layer 5 — Your Long-Term Empire
(The version of you making $10K, $30K, $100K+ months)

This workbook helps you build all five layers.

Your ideas become architecture. Your strengths become offers. Your purpose becomes a brand. Your identity becomes your business model. You are not building a small business. You are building a legacy.

WHY MOST BUSINESS MODELS FAIL

They fail because they are:

- too complicated
- not aligned
- not sustainable
- not built around strengths
- not designed around energy
- built from pressure
- built from comparison
- built without a long-term map

Women don't fail because they're not capable. They fail because the model was wrong for them. This step prevents that.

THE FIVE LAYERS OF A PROFITABLE EMPIRE

This is the deeper, expanded version, the true business architecture behind Step 4.

Most women start their business with content.
Or with a niche. Or with a logo. Or with a half-formed offer.

But a real empire, the kind that grows, sustains, evolves, and scales, is built on **five structural pillars.** These are the foundations of a business that lasts. A business that feels aligned. A business that can grow with you instead of collapsing under you. Step 4 helps you design all five with clarity. Here is what they truly mean:

1. YOUR SIGNATURE CORE OFFER

Your transformation. Your brilliance. Your anchor.

This is the offer your brand is built around the one that expresses your purpose, your genius, and your identity. Your signature offer is:
- the transformation you're uniquely designed to guide
- the clearest expression of your skill + purpose + personality
- the "end result" someone hires you for
- the center of your ecosystem
- the offer that shapes your business model
- the anchor that builds brand authority

Your signature offer should feel:
- natural
- true
- exciting
- sustainable
- aligned
- like a direct expression of who you are

It is not a forced container. It is the purest channel of your gifts. This is the offer that creates the ripple effect. the one your digital products, services, funnels, and brand all orbit around. This is your anchor.

2. YOUR DIGITAL PRODUCT ECOSYSTEM

Scalable income. Passive revenue. Creative expression.

Digital products are the **multiplication** of your brilliance.

They turn one idea into income that grows without additional labor.
They allow people to access your wisdom at accessible price points.
They build trust, authority, and momentum inside your brand.

Your digital product ecosystem should feel:
- creative
- fun
- light
- scalable
- diverse
- aligned with your message
- representative of your range

This ecosystem includes:
- entry-level products
- mid-tier products
- signature digital programs
- premium digital bundles
- evergreen products

Each digital product solves a piece of the larger transformation from your core offer.

Digital products give your business:
- passive income
- more reach
- more options for buyers
- more authority
- more ways for people to say yes
- more freedom for you

This is how your empire begins to scale *beyond* your time.

3. YOUR RECURRING REVENUE

Predictability. Stability. Freedom.

Recurring revenue is the **financial nervous system** of your business.
It stabilizes your income. It stabilizes your emotions. It stabilizes your growth. It stabilizes your ability to scale without panic.

Recurring revenue removes the rollercoaster.
It gives you space to breathe. To create. To rest. To plan like a CEO instead of surviving like a freelancer.

Recurring revenue can come from:
- memberships
- subscriptions
- monthly retainers
- recurring services
- ongoing support containers
- digital libraries
- content vaults
- community-based offerings

Your recurring revenue should be built around:
- what feels sustainable for you to deliver
- what provides ongoing value to your audience
- what fits your energy and lifestyle
- what creates stability without pressure

Recurring revenue is the **foundation of your freedom.**

It's the income that shows up every month, even if life gets chaotic. Even if you take a break. Even if you stop selling for a moment. This is what makes your empire feel safe.

4. YOUR BRAND IDENTITY SYSTEM

Your voice. Your message. Your market position.

Your brand identity is more than aesthetics.
It's how people feel around you.
It's how they understand you.
It's how they recognize you.
It's how they trust you.

Your brand identity is made of:
- your voice
- your tone
- your message
- your values
- your positioning
- your story
- your emotional resonance

It answers the questions:
- Who am I in this industry?
- What do I stand for?
- Why should someone follow me?
- Why should someone trust me?

- What makes me impossible to compare?
- Why does my work matter?

Your brand identity is the **magnet** of your business.
It draws in the people meant for you.
It filters out the ones who aren't.

When your brand identity is aligned, your content becomes easier, your marketing becomes clearer, your offer becomes stronger, and your message becomes unmistakable. This is the soul of your empire.

5. YOUR LONG-TERM EMPIRE VISION

Where this is going. What this becomes.
What you ultimately want to be known for.

Your long-term vision is the **north star** of your entire business ecosystem.

It clarifies your direction so you don't create random offers, burn yourself out, or wander into someone else's lane.

Your empire vision holds:
- the brand you're building toward
- the identity you are stepping into
- the legacy you're creating
- the message you want to embody
- the revenue level you're headed for
- the lifestyle you desire
- the evolution of your work
- the mark you will leave

This vision shapes:
- your pricing
- your marketing
- your funnel
- your business model
- your product suite
- your creative direction
- your lifestyle choices
- your future offers

This is the blueprint of everything you will become. This is where you step into your next identity. Your next level. Your future empire.

CONCLUSION

These five foundations form the architecture of your business. When they are aligned, your empire isn't something you chase, it's something you grow into with ease. And Step 4 helps you build all five.

WHAT YOU'RE BUILDING IN STEP 4

By the end of Step 4, you will have:
- a signature offer
- a product suite
- 3–7 digital products
- aligned services
- recurring revenue streams
- your brand message
- your marketing direction
- your long-term business identity
- your empire blueprint
- your entire business ecosystem mapped

Every single piece will fit your:
- skills
- energy
- purpose
- income goals
- personality
- values
- lifestyle

This is your architecture.

THE EMPIRE MAP METHOD

To build your business ecosystem, use this simple sequence:

STEP 1 — Clarify your core offer.

What is the transformation you help create?

_____

_____

STEP 2 — Build supporting digital products.

What solves pieces of the same problem?

_____

_____

STEP 3 — Add your aligned services.

What do people naturally come to you for?

_____

_____

STEP 4 — Build recurring revenue.

How do you support people ongoing?

_____

_____

STEP 5 — Map your brand identity.

How do you want to be seen?

_____

_____

STEP 6 — Envision your long-term empire.

Who are you becoming as you scale?

_____

_____

YOUR SIGNATURE OFFER IDENTITY

Who I help:

_____

The problem they have:

_____

The transformation I provide:

_____

Why I'm uniquely built for this:

_____

What my offer solves:

_____

What my offer promises:

_____

_____

YOUR DIGITAL PRODUCT ECOSYSTEM

$9–$49 Products (Entry Tier):

_____

$49–$149 Products (Growth Tier):

_____

$149–$399 Products (Signature Digital):

_____

$399–$999 Products (Premium Digital):

_____

Evergreen Products:

_____

_____

_____

_____

_____

MARKET & NICHE CLARITY PROMPTS

How to Use These Prompts

Your niche is not your limitation, it's your direction. Use these prompts to find the market where your brilliance fits effortlessly.

3-Step Method
1. Ask AI to explore niches based on your purpose and skills.
2. Identify the people who need your transformation most.
3. Choose the niche that feels like home, not a box.

PROMPTS
1. "Based on my personality, strengths, purpose, and skillset, what niches would I thrive in and why?"
2. "What niche aligns most with my natural way of communicating?"
3. "What niche would value the transformation I'm best at delivering?"
4. "What groups of people are actively struggling with the problem I'm designed to solve?"
5. "What audience would get the fastest, easiest results from my help?"
6. "What niche combines my lived experience, purpose, and expertise?"
7. "Who is already drawn to me — and what problem are they silently asking me to solve?"
8. "What niche allows me to differentiate myself effortlessly?"
9. "What niche gives me the biggest blue ocean, where I can be in a category of one?"
10. "What audience feels the most inspiring, energizing, and natural for me to serve long-term?"

BONUS REFINEMENT PROMPT

"Combine the niches above into one refined, aligned market that only I can serve and describe my role in it."

MY NICHE CLARITY SNAPSHOT

1. What I'm naturally drawn to:

_____

2. Who I feel called to help:

_____

3. What problem I'm best at solving:

_____

4. My aligned niche (initial draft):

_____

_____

5. My aligned niche (refined + simplified):

_____

_____

OFFER CREATION PROMPTS

"Prompts to map your signature offer, services, and transformation."

How to Use These Prompts

Your signature offer is the backbone of your business.

Use these prompts to design offers that:
- align with your purpose
- match your skills
- fit your energy
- serve your ideal client
- create meaningful results
- are easy for you to deliver

3-Step Method

1. Ask AI to generate offer ideas based on *who you are.*
2. Circle what feels aligned and exciting.
3. Build your signature offer from the pieces that feel true.

PROMPTS

1. "What would my signature offer be based on my strengths and purpose?"

2. "What transformation could my offer help someone achieve?"

3. "What 3–5 services match my skills and energy?"

4. "What type of client am I naturally built to help?"

5. "What problems do I solve better than most?"

6. "What would my $97, $297, and $997 offers be?"

7. "What would a premium $3,000–$10,000 offer look like for me?"

8. "What simple offer could I launch in the next 7 days?"

9. "What offer feels natural for my personality and lifestyle?"

10. "If my purpose was an offer, what would it be?"

SIGNATURE OFFER BLUEPRINT

Design Your Core, High-Impact Offer

Your signature offer is the **heart** of your business. It is the transformation you are built for. Use this worksheet to define it with clarity and alignment.

1. WHO I HELP? *Describe your ideal client in a sentence or two.*

_____

_____

2. THE CORE PROBLEM THEY STRUGGLE WITH. *What are they trying to fix, change, or understand?*

_____

_____

3. THE TRANSFORMATION I PROVIDE. *What changes because of your offer?*

_____

_____

4. WHY I'M UNIQUELY BUILT FOR THIS. *Your strengths, lived experiences, personality, purpose.*

_____

_____

5. WHAT MY OFFER INCLUDES
(Structure, format, support, modules, outcomes)

_____

_____

6. THE PROMISE OF MY OFFER
A clear statement of what they walk away with.

_____

_____

7. ALIGNED PRICE POINT
$_____ feels true in my body

_____

_____

Offer Suite Prompts

How to Use These Prompts

Your offer suite turns your idea into an ecosystem. Use these prompts to design offers that naturally stack and grow.

3-Step Method

1. Ask AI to map offers that support your signature offer.
2. Sort them into entry, mid, and premium tiers.
3. Build a suite that supports the complete transformation.

PROMPTS

Turn your idea into an ecosystem.

1. "Based on my signature offer, what natural entry-level offers should I create?"

2. "What mid-tier offers would help clients progress toward the final transformation?"

3. "What premium-level offer expresses the fullest version of my genius?"

4. "What problems does my signature offer solve — and how can each piece become its own offer?"

5. "What offer would create the quickest win for my ideal client?"

6. "What offer would give them the deepest transformation?"

7. "What offers would create a natural 1–2–3 progression?"

8. "What offers would let someone work with me at any budget?"

9. "How can I turn my framework into a full ecosystem of solutions?"

10. "What gaps exist in my industry and how can my offer suite fill them?"

BONUS REFINEMENT PROMPT

"Design my complete offer suite in a stacked ladder: entry → mid → signature → premium."

DIGITAL PRODUCT PROMPTS

"Prompts to create scalable, passive income products unique to you."

How to Use These Prompts

Digital products turn your ideas into income that grows even when you're not working.

Use these prompts to find products that feel:
- Creative
- Fun
- Light
- On-brand
- Unique
- Sustainable
- Profitable

3-Step Method
1. Ask AI to map digital products to your strengths.
2. Choose the easiest and most exciting.
3. Build your first product suite.

PROMPTS

1. "What digital products fit my personality and skills?"

2. "What digital products could I create quickly?"

3. "What templates, guides, or resources could I sell?"

4. "What digital products match my niche?"

5. "What low-ticket products could build my audience?"

6. "What mid-ticket digital products could scale?"

7. "What premium digital products could I create?"

8. "What problems can I solve with a digital resource?"

9. "What products match my long-term brand direction?"

10. "What digital products could become evergreen income?"

WORKSHEET:
DIGITAL PRODUCT SUITE MAP

Create Scalable, Evergreen Income

Your digital products are your **passive income, creative expression, and brand expansion.** Use this worksheet to build a complete digital product ecosystem.

ENTRY TIER PRODUCTS ($9–$49)
Quick wins, lead generators, beginner-friendly resources.

_____

_____

GROWTH TIER PRODUCTS ($49–$149)
More depth, more transformation, more value.

_____

_____

SIGNATURE DIGITAL PRODUCTS ($149–$399)
Your polished, high-value, evergreen staples.

_____

_____

PREMIUM DIGITAL PRODUCTS ($399–$999)
Advanced, comprehensive digital programs or bundles.

_____

_____

EVERGREEN PRODUCTS
What sells consistently, year-round, without heavy maintenance?

_____

_____

WHICH PRODUCTS FEEL LIGHT, FUN, AND ALIGNED TO RELEASE FIRST?

_____

_____

SERVICE OFFER PROMPTS

"Prompts to build services aligned with your natural gifts."

How to Use These Prompts

Services are your fastest path to income because you're monetizing what you already know.

Use these prompts to find services that feel:
- Natural
- Valuable
- Sustainable
- Aligned
- Profitable

3-Step Method
1. Ask AI to map services to your skills.
2. Choose the ones that feel light, not draining.
3. Build 1–2 service offerings to start.

PROMPTS

1. "What service-based offers match my strengths?"

2. "What do people already come to me for?"

3. "What 3 services could I launch immediately?"

4. "What high-value service could I offer?"

5. "What would my VIP service include?"

6. "What skills of mine translate into service-based income?"

7. "How could I package my skills into simple services?"

8. "What client transformation am I uniquely built for?"

9. "What service would be fun and natural for me to deliver?"

10. "What would my signature service be?"

WORKSHEET: ALIGNED SERVICE DESIGN

Build Services That Match Your Strengths + Energy

Services are your **fastest path to cash flow**, but they must be aligned with how you naturally work.

1. WHAT I AM NATURALLY GOOD AT (SKILLS)

2. WHAT PEOPLE ALREADY COME TO ME FOR

3. MY LOW-TICKET SERVICES ($97–$297). *Quick-win service offerings.*

4. MY MID-TICKET SERVICES ($300–$1,000). *More depth or support.*

5. MY PREMIUM SERVICES ($1,000+)
Deep, high-touch, highly transformational.

6. MY VIP EXPERIENCE
If someone paid for the BEST version of me, what would that include?

7. SERVICE BOUNDARIES & ENERGY NEEDS
Hours, communication style, delivery style.

RECURRING REVENUE PROMPTS

"Prompts to build subscriptions, memberships, retainers, and monthly income streams."

How to Use These Prompts

Recurring revenue gives you financial stability
so you can scale without panic.

Use these prompts to build predictable income you can count on.

3-Step Method
1. Ask AI to match recurring income to your lifestyle.
2. Choose options that feel sustainable.
3. Build one recurring offer to anchor your income.

PROMPTS

1. "What recurring revenue options fit my lifestyle?"

2. "What membership could I create based on my skills?"

3. "What subscription products match my gifts?"

4. "What could I offer monthly that provides ongoing value?"

5. "What kind of community could I lead?"

6. "What would my $20/month recurring offer be?"

7. "What would my $100–$300/month offer be?"

8. "What simple subscription service could I run?"

9. "What could I offer as a monthly retainer?"

10. "What recurring revenue model aligns with my energy?"

WORKSHEET:
RECURRING REVENUE BUILDER

Design Monthly Income You Can Count On

Recurring revenue = predictable income + emotional safety.
These are the offers that stabilize your business.

1. MEMBERSHIP IDEAS. *Community, education, accountability, coaching.*

_____

_____

2. SUBSCRIPTIONS. *Digital products, templates, content, tools.*

_____

_____

3. RETAINERS. *Monthly clients, done-for-you services, maintenance.*

_____

_____

4. MONTHLY DIGITAL DELIVERY
What could you send/update monthly?

_____

_____

5. WHAT FEELS SUSTAINABLE FOR MY ENERGY?

_____

_____

6. MY MONTHLY INCOME GOAL

$_____ per month

7. MY RECURRING REVENUE PLAN TO MEET THAT GOAL

_____

_____

_____

BRAND IDENTITY PROMPTS

How to Use These Prompts

Your brand identity is the emotional fingerprint of your business.

Use these prompts to design a brand that feels like *you*, unmistakable and magnetic.

3-Step Method

1. Ask AI to define your voice, message, and tone.
2. Identify what makes you different from anyone else in your industry.
3. Build a brand identity around your truth, not the trends.

PROMPTS

1. "What is the essence of my brand?"

2. "What emotions do I want my brand to evoke?"

3. "What words define my brand identity?"

4. "What aesthetic matches my energy?"

5. "What is my unique position in the market?"

6. "What does my brand stand for?"

7. "What is the long-term vision behind my brand?"

8. "What makes my voice different?"

9. "What niche naturally fits me?"

10. "What brand would my future CEO self build?"

WORKSHEET:
BRAND IDENTITY BLUEPRINT

Craft the Brand You're Growing Into

Your brand is not just visuals, it is your voice, your essence, your energy, your presence.

1. BRAND ESSENCE (3–6 WORDS)
The soul of your brand.

_____

2. BRAND EMOTIONS (HOW YOU WANT PEOPLE TO FEEL)

_____

_____

3. BRAND VALUES

_____

_____

4. BRAND PERSONALITY. *Soft? Bold? Precise? Spiritual? Direct? Elegant? Edgy?*

_____

_____

5. BRAND MESSAGING (YOUR CORE STATEMENT)
What you stand for + who you help + the transformation you guide.

_____

_____

6. BRAND AESTHETIC. *Visuals, colors, fonts, mood, vibe.*

_____

_____

7. LONG-TERM BRAND IDENTITY (5–10 YEARS OUT)

_____

_____

_____

MARKETING & MESSAGING PROMPTS

How to Use These Prompts
Your message is the bridge between your brilliance and the people who need it.
Use these prompts to clarify what you stand for and why it matters.

3-Step Method
1. Tell AI who you help and what you believe in.
2. Refine your message until it feels crisp and true.
3. Build your positioning around the transformation you create.

PROMPTS

1. "What is the simplest, most natural marketing style for me?"

2. "What content topics fit my energy and offer?"

3. "What is my brand message in one sentence?"

4. "What stories does my ideal client need to hear?"

5. "What messaging communicates my transformation clearly?"

6. "What content pillars match my brand identity?"

7. "What platform suits my natural strengths?"

8. "What type of content makes selling easy for me?"

9. "What marketing flows fit my lifestyle?"

10. "What is the simplest marketing plan for my first 90 days?"

TEACHING PAGE:
CREATING YOUR BLUE OCEAN
THE MARKET WHERE YOU HAVE NO COMPETITION

Most women build their business in the red ocean:
crowded markets, underpriced offers, comparison, and exhaustion.

But you're not here to compete.
You're here to **create a category of one**.

A *blue ocean* business is one where:

• you are incomparable
• your offer stands alone
• your message is distinct
• your value is unmistakable
• people choose you because no one else feels like you

You don't dominate an industry.
You create a *new lane* inside it.

The key idea behind your Blue Ocean Strategy:

No one can compete with you when your business is built from your identity, not your industry.

In Step 4, we're not just mapping offers, we're mapping your **un-copyable space**.

This is the moment your business stops being "one of many"
and becomes **the only one doing it like you.**

If you haven't read the book, I highly suggest doing so.

BLUE OCEAN POSITIONING MAP

Use this page to identify what makes your business uniquely YOU,
your differentiation, your edge, your category of one.

1. WHAT I DO DIFFERENTLY FROM EVERYONE ELSE

_____

_____

2. WHAT I REFUSE TO DO LIKE THE INDUSTRY

_____

_____

3. WHAT MY CLIENT GETS HERE THAT THEY CAN'T GET ANYWHERE ELSE

_____

_____

4. MY UN-COPYABLE ELEMENT (THE PIECE NO ONE CAN REPLICATE)

_____

_____

5. HOW I MAKE THE COMPETITION IRRELEVANT

_____

_____

6. WHAT MAKES WORKING WITH ME A NEW EXPERIENCE

_____

_____

_____

BLUE OCEAN IDEA PROMPTS

How to Use These Prompts
Your Blue Ocean is the space where you have no competition.
Use these prompts to define your category of one.

3-Step Method
1. Ask AI what makes your work uncopyable.
2. Identify what you refuse to do like the industry.
3. Build a lane so unique the competition becomes irrelevant.

Prompts to help AI map your *unique lane*: your market, message, offer, and identity that stand alone.

1. "What is my Blue Ocean, the space where I have no competition?"

2. "How is my offer different from everything else in the industry?"

3. "What unique combination of skills, personality, and purpose creates my category of one?"

4. "What am I doing that no one else is doing or no one else is doing *this way*?"

5. "What is the unique experience someone gets working with me?"

6. "How can I reframe my niche so it becomes uniquely mine?"

7. "How does my purpose create my differentiation?"

8. "What industry norms am I breaking and why does that make me valuable?"

9. "How can I position my offer so it stands alone in the market?"

10. "What brand angle could I claim that automatically makes my competitors irrelevant?"

Content Strategy Prompts

How to Use These Prompts

Content is the engine that moves your message through the world. Use these prompts to build a content plan that attracts, nurtures, and converts.

3-Step Method
1. Ask AI to match content styles to your energy and platform.
2. Identify the core messages your audience needs.
3. Build a rhythm that feels sustainable and magnetic.

PROMPTS

Build content that attracts, nurtures, and converts.

1. "What content pillars align with my message, audience, and signature offer?"
2. "What content formats best match my natural energy and communication style?"
3. "What content would build trust with my exact ideal client?"
4. "What content would position me as an authority in my lane?"
5. "What content solves problems my audience has right now?"
6. "What educational content leads people naturally into my offers?"
7. "What storytelling content builds emotional resonance?"
8. "What content attracts my soulmate clients effortlessly?"
9. "What content do I love creating that also grows my audience?"
10. "What content creates demand for my signature offer?"

BONUS PROMPTS:
"Turn my message into a 30-day content plan built around clarity, value, and conversion."

Visibility & Growth Prompts

How to Use These Prompts

Visibility is not about being everywhere, it's about being unforgettable.
Use these prompts to grow your audience in aligned, sustainable ways.

3-Step Method
1. Tell AI your preferred platforms and strengths.
2. Ask for visibility strategies that match your personality.
3. Choose the easiest strategy that creates the biggest ripple.

PROMPTS

Be unforgettable, not overwhelmed.

1. "Based on my strengths, what visibility strategies fit me best?"
2. "What platforms would grow my audience with the least resistance?"
3. "What visibility methods align with my personality and energy?"
4. "What growth strategies will attract the right people, not just more people?"
5. "What small consistent actions would compound my visibility?"

6. "What collaborations or cross-promotions would benefit my audience?"
7. "What type of content makes me naturally discoverable?"
8. "What unique angles or messages make me stand out online?"
9. "What's my easiest route to 10K followers?"
10. "What's my simplest visibility plan for the next 90 days?"

Bonus Prompt:
"Design a low-effort, high-impact visibility strategy tailored to my strengths."

FUNNEL & CUSTOMER JOURNEY PROMPTS

How to Use These Prompts
A funnel automates trust, desire, and sales.
Use these prompts to create a simple, high-converting system.

3-Step Method
1. Ask AI to outline the ideal funnel for your offer.
2. Choose the path that feels simplest and most aligned.
3. Build one funnel, then expand your empire.

PROMPTS
1. "What would my customer journey look like from first contact to transformation?"
2. "What freebie or lead magnet matches my offer?"
3. "What simple funnel could I build with my current skills?"
4. "What 3-step pathway leads someone into my signature offer?"
5. "What type of content builds trust with my client?"
6. "What automated pathway could make sales easier for me?"
7. "What nurturing sequence matches my brand voice?"
8. "What is the simplest funnel for my personality?"
9. "What repeatable system would increase conversions?"
10. "What funnel would create passive or semi-passive sales for me?"

Sales Flow Prompts

How to Use These Prompts

Selling is simply helping someone step into their next level.

Use these prompts to create ease, confidence, and clarity in your sales process.

3-Step Method

1. Ask AI to define your natural sales style.
2. Identify friction points and remove them.
3. Build a sales flow that feels human, ethical, and effective.

PROMPTS

Selling with ease, clarity, and humanity.

1. "Based on my personality, what is my natural sales style?"
2. "How can I create a sales process that feels supportive, not pushy?"
3. "What beliefs about selling do I need to shift?"
4. "What does my ideal client need to hear before they buy?"
5. "What objections do I solve naturally through my work?"
6. "How can my content pre-sell my offers automatically?"
7. "What sales journey leads someone from first touch to purchase?"
8. "What simple sales rhythm can I use weekly?"
9. "What high-converting CTA matches my voice?"
10. "What friction points do I need to remove from my sales process?"

BONUS REFINEMENT PROMPT:

"Create my full aligned sales flow: awareness → nurturing → desire → purchase."

PRICING & MONETIZATION PROMPTS

How to Use These Prompts

Your pricing should feel aligned, abundant, and grounded in value.

Use these prompts to create a pricing model that supports your goals.

3-Step Method

1. Ask AI to map pricing options based on value and demand.
2. Choose the tiered structure that feels empowering.
3. Build a ladder that naturally leads to your signature offer.

PROMPTS

1. "What is the aligned pricing for each of my offers?"
2. "What would my value-based pricing look like?"
3. "How can I structure tiered pricing?"
4. "What would my high-ticket offer include?"
5. "What monetization strategies match my strengths?"

6. "How can I make income more predictable?"
7. "What premium version of my offer could I create?"
8. "What value am I undercharging for?"
9. "What prices feel aligned in my body?"
10. "What pricing supports the lifestyle I want?"

Wealth & Income Path Prompts

How to Use These Prompts
Your income grows when your clarity grows.
Use these prompts to map pathways to $10K, $30K, $100K, and beyond.

3-Step Method
1. Ask AI to reverse-engineer your income goals.
2. Choose the simplest path that aligns with your strengths.
3. Build one clear revenue plan and commit.

PROMPTS
Map your path to $10K, $30K, $100K, and beyond.

1. "What is the simplest path to $10K/month with my current skillset?"
2. "What's the scalable path to $30K/month?"
3. "What revenue streams get me to $100K/year the fastest?"
4. "What leverage points can increase my income without more hours?"
5. "What bottlenecks do I need to remove to grow?"
6. "What pricing adjustments would align my income with my value?"
7. "What offers should I prioritize based on income momentum?"
8. "Where am I undercharging or overdelivering?"
9. "How can I create income predictability each month?"
10. "What would my millionaire path look like?"

BONUS REFINEMENT PROMPT:
"Reverse-engineer my next income milestone based on my strengths and lifestyle."

CEO Identity Prompts

How to Use These Prompts
Your business can only expand to the level of your identity.
Use these prompts to step into the version of you who leads an empire.

3-Step Method
1. Ask AI to help you define your CEO identity.
2. Identify the habits, boundaries, and mindset she lives by.
3. Practice becoming her one intentional step at a time.

PROMPTS
Step into the identity that leads the empire.

1. "Who is the CEO version of me and how does she think?"
2. "What habits support the CEO identity I'm stepping into?"
3. "What boundaries does she hold without apology?"
4. "What does she no longer tolerate?"
5. "What systems does she rely on instead of willpower?"
6. "What decisions does she make quickly?"
7. "What does she do daily, weekly, and monthly as a leader?"
8. "What is her relationship to money, time, and energy?"
9. "How does she handle challenges, launches, and visibility?"
10. "How can I embody her today in one small action?"

BONUS REFINEMENT PROMPT:
"Write my CEO identity blueprint: mindset, habits, standards, and behaviors."

BRAND FUTURE & LONG-TERM EMPIRE PROMPTS
"Prompts to imagine the brand you're becoming and build toward it."

How to Use These Prompts

Your long-term empire begins with the brand identity you choose now. These prompts help you create a business that grows with you, not out of you.

3-Step Method
1. Ask AI to explore the future version of your work.
2. Identify the evolution your business naturally wants to take.
3. Build a vision big enough to grow into.

Your empire is not built in a day it's built from direction. Use these prompts to map the brand, impact, and legacy you're creating.

PROMPTS
Build the brand, legacy, and future you're meant for.

1. "What long-term brand could this grow into?"
2. "What would my business look like at $10K/month?"
3. "What would it look like at $30K/month?"
4. "What would it look like at $100K/month?"
5. "What would my future CEO identity build?"
6. "What is the larger mission behind my business?"
7. "What is the future empire version of this idea?"
8. "How could this evolve into a thriving brand?"
9. "What legacy business am I creating?"
10. "What is my long-term empire vision?"
11. "What is the ultimate evolution of my brand?"

12. "What do I want to be known for in 5+ years?"
13. "What programs, books, products, or frameworks could grow from this?"
14. "What is the deeper mission beneath my work?"
15. "How does my business impact people long-term?"
16. "How will my offer suite evolve as I evolve?"
17. "What does my empire look like when it's fully built?"
18. "What identity am I growing into?"
19. "What does my dream business feel like day to day?"
20. "What is the legacy I'm creating through this?"

BONUS REFINEMENT PROMPT:

"Describe my fully realized empire: the brand, the offers, the message, the lifestyle, the impact."

WORKSHEET:
YOUR EMPIRE FUTURE MAP

Build the 5–10 Year Vision Behind Your Work

This is your **legacy**, your **destination**, your **future identity**.

1. WHO I AM IN MY EMPIRE ERA

Describe the highest, most aligned version of yourself.

_____

_____

2. WHAT MY BUSINESS LOOKS LIKE AT $10K/MONTH

_____

_____

3. WHAT IT LOOKS LIKE AT $30K/MONTH

_____

_____

4. WHAT IT LOOKS LIKE AT $100K/MONTH

_____

_____

5. WHAT I AM KNOWN FOR IN THE FUTURE

_____

_____

6. MY 10-YEAR EMPIRE VISION

This is where the chapter becomes destiny.

_____

_____

_____

INTEGRATION PAGE:
YOUR EMPIRE SNAPSHOT

Summarize Everything You Built in Step 4

This brings all worksheets together into ONE clear business map.

MY SIGNATURE OFFER

MY SECONDARY OFFERS

MY DIGITAL PRODUCTS

MY PRODUCT SUITE

.

MY SERVICES

MY RECURRING INCOME STREAMS

MY BRAND IDENTITY

_____

_____

IDEAL CLIENT & TRANSFORMATION

_____

_____

MARKETING STYLE

_____

_____

LONG-TERM BRAND DIRECTION

_____

_____

MY FUTURE EMPIRE VISION (5-10 YEARS)

_____

_____

WHAT I'M BUILDING FIRST:

_____

_____

WHY THIS FEELS ALIGNED:

_____

_____

INTEGRATION REFLECTION

This is the moment where clarity becomes direction.

Step 4 gave you ideas, structure, offers, brand identity, and the blueprint of your empire, but integration is where everything starts to *land* in your body.

Use this page to slow down, breathe, and connect with what feels true.

These questions are designed to help you:
- recognize the pieces that feel aligned
- let go of anything that feels heavy or forced
- choose what to build first
- listen to the signals from your intuition, not pressure
- anchor into the empire you're starting to see

Answer honestly.
Answer slowly.
Answer without obligation.

Your alignment is the strategy.
Your intuition is the roadmap.
Your excitement is the direction.

Let this page reveal what's next: naturally, clearly, effortlessly.

What feels most aligned from this step?

What empire am I starting to see?

What feels exciting to build first?

What feels like a full-body yes?

EMPIRE COMMITMENT PAGE

I am building a business that fits my life, not a business I have to fight to sustain.

I choose alignment over pressure.

I choose clarity over chaos.

I choose my truth over comparison.

I choose to build with intention, purpose, and power.

My empire begins with one aligned step.

Signed,

The woman becoming her future self

CLOSING NOTE

This step is your blueprint.
Your architecture.
Your foundation.

You are no longer guessing your way into a business.
You are designing it: intentionally, intelligently, and aligned with who you are.

Your purpose lives in Step 2.
Your ideas came alive in Step 3.
Your empire begins here in Step 4.

And in Step 5…
we turn this into a real business plan.

STEP 5:
THE BUSINESS PLAN BUILDER

"Prompts to Build a Full AI-Generated Business Plan"

This is the moment where everything begins to take shape. You've explored your purpose, clarified your ideas, and mapped the roots of your empire. Now you're ready to bring it all forward: intentionally, clearly, and powerfully.

Step 5 isn't about creating a rigid corporate document. It's about creating a business plan that feels like **alignment, direction, and self-trust**.

A plan that reflects your voice, your values, and the woman you're becoming.

This step helps you use AI as your strategic partner to articulate your brand, define your market, shape your offers, and outline a pathway that feels like it was made for you.

Not rushed. Not overwhelming. Simply clear.

WELCOME

This is the sexy part. This is where everything you uncovered in Steps 1–4 becomes a real, structured, million-dollar business plan.

You're not just "starting a business."
You're architecting an empire that fits your identity, energy, and desired life.

Most women never write a business plan. They either:
- drown in ideas with no direction
- build offers with no ecosystem
- hustle content with no strategy
- improvise "their brand" every week

Step 5 changes that.

This step teaches you to use AI as your:
- personal business strategist
- funnel architect
- marketing and sales planner
- monetization partner
- scaling advisor

You'll walk away with:
- a clear business model
- your target market and ideal client
- a full offer + product suite

- your brand positioning + content pillars
- a simple funnel and sales system
- an email + nurture plan
- a launch plan
- a 12-month roadmap
- weekly milestones and revenue goals
- mindset + habit prompts to execute like a seven-figure entrepreneur

Your goal is not to write a perfect corporate deck.

Your goal is to build a lean, high-leverage, ruthlessly effective plan that feels like a cheat code.

HOW TO USE THIS STEP

Every prompt in Step 5 is designed to give AI context so it can "think like your strategist," not like a generic business blogger.

Use it like this:

1. **Choose a section** (Business Model, Target Audience, Funnel, etc.).
2. **Copy 1–3 prompts** into AI.
3. At the top, add this instruction:

"Act as my personal business strategist. Base your answers on everything I've already discovered in Steps 1–4 of The AI Empire Builder (my identity, purpose, strengths, energy, ideas, and empire map). Create clear, practical, step-by-step guidance, not fluff."

4. **Read slowly.** Highlight what feels:
   o aligned
   o exciting
   o doable
   o like "oh my god, that's me"
5. **Edit and personalize.** This is *your* plan, not AI's.
6. **Turn insight into action.** For every section, choose:
   o one decision
   o one next step

By the end of this step, you'll have a fully AI-assisted business plan that was actually built around you.

TEACHING PAGE:
THE TRUTH ABOUT A BUSINESS PLAN

Your business plan is not:
- a 40-page investor document
- a corporate template
- a rigid, never-changing PDF

Your business plan **is**:
- a living blueprint
- a decision document
- a pattern of priorities
- a commitment to how you build, sell, and scale

A powerful plan answers 7 core questions:

1. Who am I as a founder and what kind of business fits me?

2. Who do I serve and what problem am I built to solve?

3. What is my leanest, most aligned business model?

4. What offers, products, and price points make up my ecosystem?

5. How will I attract, nurture, and convert my audience?

6. How will this business make money in the next 12 months?

7. Who do I need to become to execute this without burning out?

Step 5 walks you through each of these using AI as your co-strategist.

You are not guessing.
You are choosing.
You are architecting your first million.

SECTION 1
FOUNDER & BUSINESS IDENTITY SNAPSHOT

"Prompts to define who you are as a founder and what kind of business you're building."

HOW TO USE THESE PROMPTS

1. Paste 2–3 prompts into AI.
2. Ask AI to answer as if it's your **personal strategist + future CEO self**.
3. Turn the answers into a one-page "Founder Snapshot" at the end.

PROMPTS

1. "Summarize who I am as a founder based on my purpose, strengths, energy, and archetypes from Steps 1–4. Describe my natural leadership, creative style, and decision-making."

2. "What type of digital business model best fits my personality, nervous system, and lifestyle (content-driven, low-overhead, scalable, no tech overwhelm)?"

3. "Describe my ideal role inside my business: what I actually want to spend most of my time doing vs. what should eventually be automated or delegated."

4. "Based on my strengths and patterns, what kind of CEO am I designed to become in the next 3 years?"

5. "What business environments, schedules, and structures support my best work?"

6. "What do I *not* want in my business (non-negotiables, hard no's, red flags)?"

7. "Write a one-paragraph 'Founder Bio' for the front page of my business plan that captures who I am, what I care about, and what I'm building."

8. "Turn my strengths and lived experience into a short 'Why I'm Built For This' section for my business plan."

WORKSHEET:

FOUNDER SNAPSHOT

Fill this out after you run the prompts.

Who I Am as a Founder (3–5 sentences):

_____

_____

_____

_____

My Natural Role in the Business:

_____

_____

What I'm Building (in one sentence):

_____

_____

Non-Negotiables (what I refuse to tolerate in my business):

_____

_____

_____

Why I'm Built for This:

_____

_____

_____

SECTION 2
LEAN MILLION-DOLLAR BUSINESS MODEL

"Prompts to choose the simplest model that can realistically reach $1M in 12–36 months."

TEACHING

You don't hit seven figures by stacking random offers. You hit seven figures by choosing **one primary model** and committing to it:
- digital products
- courses/programs
- memberships
- services / retainers
- hybrid (services → products → membership)

Your model must match:
- your energy
- your skills
- your schedule
- your income goals

HOW TO USE THESE PROMPTS
1. Tell AI your income goals for the next 12 months (ex: $100K, $250K, $1M).
2. Use these prompts to design a **lean, high-margin model**.
3. Keep what feels aligned, discard what feels heavy.

PROMPTS
1. "Based on my strengths, lifestyle, and income goals, what is the leanest business model I can use to reach $10K/month in the next 6–12 months?"
2. "Design 3 possible business models for me (service-heavy, product-heavy, and hybrid). Show pros, cons, and which one fits my energy and goals the best."
3. "If my goal is at least $1M in revenue within 12–36 months, what business model makes the most sense for me and why?"
4. "Map out how my business model could evolve over 3 years (Year 1: cash flow and proof of concept; Year 2: scale and systems; Year 3: empire and team)."
5. "Create a simple 'one-page business model' for me: who I serve, what I sell, how I deliver it, and how the money flows."
6. "What revenue streams should be my **primary focus** vs. **secondary / later**?"
7. "What are 3 business models I should *avoid* based on my energy, time, and preferences?"

WORKSHEET:
MY BUSINESS MODEL CHOICE

This page helps you anchor the business model you're committing to for the next 12 months.
Think of it as your foundation: simple, intentional, and aligned with who you are.

This isn't about choosing the "perfect" model. It's about choosing the model that feels sustainable, spacious, and capable of growth. Use the prompts you explored in this section to complete the worksheet with clarity and confidence.

Primary Model (for the next 12 months)

Identify the single business model you want to focus on first.
Examples include:
- digital products
- memberships
- done-for-you services
- coaching or consulting
- hybrid (services → products)
  Choose the path that feels the most natural and immediately profitable for you right now.

Main Revenue Streams

List up to three income sources you'll build this year. These should be the simplest, most aligned revenue paths for your model not everything you might create someday. This keeps your focus clean and your growth intentional.

Why This Model Fits Me

Write a short explanation of why this model supports:
- your energy
- your schedule
- your strengths
- your preferred way of working
  This section helps you stay rooted in *why* you chose this model whenever doubt creeps in.

How This Model Scales to $1M+

Describe how the business model naturally expands as your audience grows.
This could include:
- adding recurring revenue
- building a premium tier
- creating a larger ecosystem of products
- increasing volume through audience expansion
- automating delivery or fulfillment
  This reminds you that your first-year model is the beginning of a much larger vision.

Primary Model (for the next 12 months):

_____

Main Revenue Streams:

1. _____

2. _____

3. _____

Why This Model Fits Me:

_____

How This Model Scales to $1M+:

_____

_____

SECTION 3
MARKET, NICHE & IDEAL CLIENT

"Prompts to lock in who you serve, what problem you solve, and how you stand out."

HOW TO USE THESE PROMPTS

1. Use your clarity from Step 2 (purpose) and Step 4 (niche prompts).
2. Run 3–5 prompts.
3. Turn the insights into a clean Ideal Client + Niche section.

PROMPTS

1. "Based on my story, strengths, and patterns, who am I most naturally built to serve in the market? Describe my ideal client in vivid detail."

2. "What urgent problems or desires does my ideal client have that I am uniquely positioned to help with?"

3. "Write a one-paragraph 'Niche Statement' that includes who I help, what problem I solve, and the outcome I guide them toward."

4. "What frustrations, fears, and dreams are driving my ideal client's buying decisions right now?"

5. "How is my ideal client currently trying to solve this problem on their own—and why isn't it working?"

6. "What makes me different from others in my niche (voice, approach, background, energy, method)?"

7. "Write a 'Category of One' positioning statement that explains why my work is incomparable in my niche."

8. "List 10 beliefs my ideal client currently holds that I need to validate or gently challenge in my marketing."

9. "List 10 phrases my ideal client would actually type into Google or say to a friend when they're struggling with this problem."

10. "Summarize my market, niche, ideal client, and positioning in one tight page for my business plan."

WORKSHEET:
MARKET & IDEAL CLIENT SNAPSHOT

My Niche (simple sentence):

_____

_____

Who I Help:

_____

Core Problem I Solve:

_____

Core Transformation / Promise:

_____

Why They Choose Me (my edge):

_____

_____

THE MARKET ORBIT
Understanding Your Competitive Landscape

Your work exists within a living ecosystem of creators, coaches, brands, and voices. Each offering their own style of transformation and support. This section isn't about comparison; it's about clarity. It helps you understand the space you're entering, the patterns your audience is already seeing, and the opportunities waiting for you.

The Landscape You're Entering

Your niche includes:
- creators teaching similar topics
- businesses offering parallel tools
- influencers shaping cultural conversations
- brands offering alternative solutions

Each one reveals a piece of what your ideal client is already consuming and what they still cannot find.

What the Market Is Missing

Most brands in your orbit tend to lack:
- emotional intelligence
- long-term depth
- personalized nuance
- a grounded feminine voice
- trauma-aware insight
- true structure vs. recycled content
- accessible entry points
- sustainable frameworks
- an authentic brand personality

Your Distinct Position

Your brand enters the market with clarity and intention:
- you lead with psychological depth
- you offer structured, practical guidance
- your tone is accessible but elevated
- your narrative is honest and feminine
- your transformation is rooted in self-trust
- your content is built for longevity
- your business model is designed for sustainability

This creates an unmistakable presence in your niche:
a brand that feels both deeply human and deeply professional.

SECTION 4
OFFERS, PRODUCTS & PRICING

"Prompts to turn your genius into a clear offer suite and aligned prices."

HOW TO USE THESE PROMPTS

You already mapped ideas and an empire ecosystem in Step 3 and Step 4.

Now you'll lock them into a **business-plan-ready offer suite**:
- entry offers
- core/signature offer
- premium / high-ticket
- supporting digital products

PROMPTS

1. "Based on my niche, strengths, and chosen business model, what should my **signature/core offer** be in the next 12 months?"
2. "Describe my signature offer in business-plan format: who it's for, what problem it solves, transformation, delivery, duration, price, and why it works."
3. "What 2–4 supporting digital products (low-ticket or mid-ticket) would naturally lead people into my signature offer?"
4. "What premium offer ($3,000–$10,000) could I eventually create for my most committed clients?"
5. "Map my offer suite into a value ladder: entry → core → premium. Show how each step deepens the transformation."
6. "What simple, low-ticket offer could I launch quickly to generate my first buyers and proof of concept?"
7. "Based on my market and transformation, suggest price ranges for my offers that feel ethical, sustainable, and capable of scaling to my income goals."
8. "Calculate sample revenue scenarios:
   – If I sell X of my low-ticket,
   – Y of my core offer, and
   – Z of my premium offer per month,
   how much do I earn?"
9. "What boundaries, scope, and delivery structures will keep my offers aligned with my energy (so I don't burn out)?"

WORKSHEET: OFFER SUITE OVERVIEW

Your offer suite is the heart of your business model. It's the structure that guides a client from first discovering your work to experiencing the deepest transformation you provide.

This worksheet helps you clarify your offers in a way that feels intentional, spacious, and aligned with your strengths not overwhelming or complicated. Think of this as designing the *pathway* your clients walk with you.

Use the insights from your prompts to complete each section with clarity and confidence.

Entry Offers (Lead-In / Low Ticket)

List the simple, low-cost or introductory offers that make it easy for new clients to enter your world. These offers should:
- give a quick win
- demonstrate your expertise
- build trust
- gently introduce your larger work

Examples: mini-courses, templates, guides, workshops, digital downloads, low-ticket memberships.

Choose 1–3 — no more. Keep this clean and focused.

Core / Signature Offer

This is the centerpiece of your business. The offer that represents the transformation you're most known for. Fill in:
- **Name** — memorable, aligned, clear
- **Price** — sustainable for you, accessible for them
- **Promise** — the core transformation or outcome you deliver

Your signature offer should feel natural to your strengths and big enough to grow with you.

Premium Offer(s)

These are your deeper, higher-level containers. They are designed for clients who want:
- more access
- more depth
- more personalization
- more transformation

Premium doesn't mean more "work" for you, it means elevated proximity, support, or experiential value.

Examples: VIP programs, intensives, retreats, private consulting, high-level memberships.

How They Stack (Entry → Core → Premium)

This explains the *client journey* through your ecosystem.

Describe:
- how your entry offers naturally lead into your core offer
- how your core offer prepares clients for your premium work
- how each offer deepens the transformation
- the logic and flow of your value ladder

This section is where your business becomes a system. A thoughtful, intuitive path that supports your clients while building predictable, scalable revenue for you.

Entry Offers (Lead-In / Low Ticket):

_____

Core / Signature Offer:

Name: _____

Price: _____

Promise: _____

Premium Offer(s):

_____

How They Stack (Entry → Core → Premium):

_____

_____

RISK ASSESSMENT & MITIGATION PLAN

Every meaningful vision carries challenges. This section exists to bring awareness, not fear, so you can lead with grounded clarity rather than reaction.

These are the risks that naturally arise when building a digital business, and the strategies that keep you steady.

1. Time & Energy Constraints

Risk: inconsistent output, low bandwidth, creative fatigue
Mitigation: batching content, pre-scheduled posts, minimalist weekly workflow, CEO days

2. Platform Dependency

Risk: algorithm shifts affecting visibility
Mitigation: build an email list, diversify platforms slowly, prioritize evergreen content

3. Early Low Sales

Risk: discouragement or premature pivots
Mitigation: consistent posting, audience education, simple entry offers, warm nurture sequences

4. Tech Overwhelm

Risk: stalling, confusion, avoidance
Mitigation: use only essential tools, automate early, choose intuitive platforms, use AI for navigation

5. Offer Misalignment

Risk: burnout, resentment, disconnection from your work
Mitigation: regular self-audits, adjust scope, redefine delivery, stay close to your strengths

6. Burnout & Overcommitment

Risk: exhaustion from urgency or pressure
Mitigation: boundaries, seasonal planning, CEO habits, simple systems, rest cycles

This plan is not about perfection.
It's about staying aware, steady, and sovereign, even when things shift.

BRAND AESTHETICS SNAPSHOT

This section helps ground your brand visually and emotionally. It's a compass for your creative direction, not rigid, simply clarifying.

Tone & Voice
- grounded
- feminine strength
- clear, compassionate, direct
- confident without force
- elevated and emotionally intelligent

Brand Essence Words
- clarity
- sovereignty
- intentional growth
- self-trust
- warm authority

Color Palette (Conceptual)
- soft neutrals
- warm earth tones
- muted pinks or rose hues
- gentle charcoal
- touches of gold for emphasis

Typography (Conceptual)
- serif for elegance
- sans-serif for clarity
- clean lines, no clutter

Imagery Style
- calm, spacious compositions
- minimal but warm environments
- subtle textures
- feminine energy without cliché
- visuals that evoke presence and depth

This aesthetic creates a brand that feels both timeless and distinctly yours.

SECTION 5
BRAND, CONTENT PILLARS & MARKETING PLAN

"Prompts to turn your voice into a clear content + visibility strategy."

HOW TO USE THESE PROMPTS

1. Decide your main platform(s): IG, TikTok, YouTube, email, blog, etc.
2. Use prompts to define your **brand message** and **content pillars**.
3. Build a simple 90-day marketing plan.

PROMPTS

1. "Describe my brand in 5–7 words (essence, tone, energy) based on everything you know about me."

2. "Write a 1–2 sentence brand message I can put at the top of my business plan: who I help, what I stand for, and the transformation I'm here to create."

3. "Create 4–6 core **content pillars** for my brand that I can post about consistently (education, story, opinion, behind-the-scenes, offers, etc.)."

4. "For each content pillar, list 10 post ideas that speak directly to my ideal client's fears, desires, and objections."

5. "Recommend 1–2 main marketing platforms I should prioritize first, based on my strengths, time, and preferences."

6. "Design a simple 90-day marketing plan using only free tools and organic content, focused on building audience and leads."

7. "Write my brand 'Do / Don't' list: what I will always do in my marketing, and what I will never do."

8. "Write a one-paragraph 'Marketing Philosophy' that reflects my values, ethics, and vibe as a business owner."

9. "Map my content to my offers: which posts lead naturally into which offer?"

WORKSHEET:
BRAND & CONTENT SNAPSHOT

Your brand is more than a color palette or a clever tagline, it's the emotional and energetic identity of your business. It's how people *feel* when they encounter your work, and the message that threads through everything you create.

This worksheet helps you translate your deeper mission into clear language, so your content becomes consistent, magnetic, and unmistakably yours. Use the insights from your prompts to fill out this page with intention and clarity. This becomes your compass for how you show up online.

Brand Essence (3–6 words)

Choose a handful of words that capture the *feeling* of your brand. These should reflect your tone, your presence, and the emotional frequency you want your audience to experience. Think:

- grounded
- bold
- refined
- compassionate
- visionary
- warm
- unapologetic

This is your brand distilled into its purest form.

Core Brand Message

Write 1–2 sentences that capture who you help, what you stand for, and the transformation your work creates. This message should feel honest, confident, and aligned with your bigger mission. It's the statement that sits at the center of your business. The line people remember you for.

Content Pillars

List 4–6 themes you will consistently speak about in your content. These pillars guide your visibility strategy and help your audience understand what your brand is about. Your content pillars might include:

- education
- storytelling
- empowerment
- behind-the-scenes
- opinion pieces
- client transformation
- mindset
- how-to guidance

Choose pillars that feel natural for your voice and supportive of your offers.

Primary Platforms

Identify the main platforms you will use to share your message and build your audience. This could include:
- Instagram
- TikTok
- YouTube
- Email
- Pinterest
- Blog

Choose the platforms that feel aligned with your energy and the type of content you enjoy creating. Consistency matters more than quantity.

This worksheet becomes the anchor for your content strategy. A simple, steady reference that keeps your voice cohesive, your message clear, and your presence recognizable across every platform.

Brand Essence (3–6 words):

_____

Core Brand Message:

_____

Content Pillars:

1. _____

2. _____

3. _____

4. _____

5. _____

Primary Platforms:

_____

_____

SECTION 6
MONETIZATION, PRICING & REVENUE PLAN

"Prompts to turn your ideas into numbers, targets, and realistic paths to income."

HOW TO USE THESE PROMPTS

1. Decide your **12-month revenue goal**.
2. Use prompts to map pricing and sales volume.
3. Keep it simple. No spreadsheets required (unless you want them).

PROMPTS

1. "Based on my offers and business model, design a simple 12-month revenue plan that gets me to $_____ in the next year."

2. "Calculate how many units of each offer I'd need to sell per month to reach $_____ / month consistently."

3. "Suggest price points for each offer that balance accessibility, sustainability, and my long-term income goals."

4. "Design 2–3 'revenue mixes' (different combinations of offers sold) that could all get me to my monthly goal."

5. "What are my most leveraged income streams and which should I prioritize first for fastest cash flow?"

6. "Where are my biggest opportunities to add **recurring revenue** (memberships, subscriptions, retainers)?"

7. "Create a one-page 'Monetization Overview' I can plug directly into my business plan: offers, price ranges, target monthly sales, and projected revenue."

WORKSHEET:
12-MONTH REVENUE SNAPSHOT

This worksheet helps you connect your vision to your numbers in a way that feels clear, simple, and empowering. It's not about pressure. It's about direction.

By mapping your income goals to your offers, you create a revenue plan that feels both achievable and aligned with your capacity.

Use this page to anchor your financial intentions for the year ahead.
Think of it as your roadmap: calm, focused, and grounded in self-trust.

Year 1 Revenue Goal

Write the total amount you want to generate in your first 12 months.

Choose a number that feels:
- expansive, yet realistic
- exciting, yet grounded
- achievable, yet motivating

This is your north star. The financial direction you are moving toward.

Target Monthly Baseline (Minimum Consistent Income)

This is the amount you want to earn consistently each month, regardless of seasonal shifts or launches.

It represents:
- stability
- safety
- breathing room
- predictable income

Your baseline supports your lifestyle and allows your creativity to flourish.

Primary Offers (Name + Price + Monthly Target Sales)

List the core offers that will generate most of your income this year. For each one, note:
- the offer name
- the price
- how many sales you aim for each month

This helps you translate your income goal into concrete, achievable sales targets.
It also clarifies where your energy should go.

Recurring Revenue Goal (If Applicable)

Recurring revenue is the foundation of long-term sustainability.
This could come from:
- memberships
- subscriptions
- retainers
- long-term programs
- ongoing digital products

Write your recurring revenue goal per month and where it will come from.
Even a small recurring stream can create significant stability in your business.

This worksheet brings financial clarity to your business plan.

It turns ideas into numbers and goals into strategy, helping you understand exactly how your business grows month by month.

Year 1 Revenue Goal:

$ _____

Target Monthly Baseline (minimum consistent income):

$ _____

Primary Offers (Name + Price + Monthly Target Sales):

_____

Recurring Revenue Goal (if applicable):

$ _____ / month from _____

_____

SECTION 7
SALES SYSTEM & SIMPLE FUNNEL

*"Prompts to design a no-drama funnel that moves people from stranger →
buyer."*

HOW TO USE THESE PROMPTS

You don't need a 14-step funnel with 12 tools.
You need a **simple path**:

Discover → Follow → Nurture → Offer → Buy

PROMPTS

1. "Design a simple, lean sales funnel for my business that does *not* require paid ads: how people discover me, get nurtured, and buy."

2. "Suggest 2–3 ideas for a lead magnet or entry offer that would attract my ideal client and naturally lead into my core offer."

3. "Describe the journey my ideal client takes from first finding me to becoming a paying client (touchpoints, content, offers)."

4. "What are the 3–5 key conversion moments in my funnel where I should focus the most energy?"

5. "What systems or automations can I set up (using AI and free tools) to make my funnel run with less manual effort?"

6. "Write a simple page for my business plan called 'How We Get Clients' that outlines my funnel in plain language."

WORKSHEET:
MY CORE FUNNEL

Your funnel is the simple, intentional pathway your audience follows from discovering your work to becoming a paying client. It doesn't need to be complicated or automated with ten different tools. A powerful funnel is grounded in clarity, consistency, and trust.

This worksheet helps you map the essential steps of your client journey so your marketing, content, and sales efforts all flow in the same direction. Think of it as designing the bridge between your audience and your offers.

Use the insights from your prompts to complete each part with ease and clarity.

Lead Source(s)

These are the platforms where new people find you for the first time. Choose 1–2 main sources to focus on. The ones that feel natural to you.

Examples:
- TikTok
- Instagram
- YouTube
- Pinterest
- Podcast interviews
- Blog posts
- Word of mouth

Clarity here keeps you from spreading yourself too thin.

Lead Magnet / Entry Offer

This is the first step someone takes toward you. It can be a free resource or a low-ticket product that gives immediate value.

Examples:
- a guide
- a checklist
- a mini-workshop
- a quiz
- a $7–$27 digital product

This offer should feel effortless for you to create and meaningful for them to receive.

Nurture Channel (Email, Social, etc.)

Once someone enters your world, this is where you build trust, relationship, and connection. Choose the channel where you can show up consistently and authentically. Examples:

- weekly email
- Instagram stories
- YouTube videos
- a private broadcast channel

Your nurture space is where your audience learns who you are and what you stand for.

Core Sales Mechanism (DMs, Calls, Sales Page, etc.)

This is the process you use to enroll people into your main offer. Choose the path that feels aligned with your energy. Examples:

- a thoughtful sales page
- a DM conversation
- a short call
- a warm email sequence
- a live workshop

Your sales mechanism should feel supportive, not stressful.

Main Offer They're Guided Into

This is the signature offer at the center of your business. The offer you ultimately want most people to enter. Write the name of the offer and the transformation it creates. This brings your entire funnel into alignment. Your funnel doesn't need complexity to be powerful. It needs flow, intention, and a clear path your audience can easily follow.

Lead Source(s):

_____

Lead Magnet / Entry Offer:

_____

Nurture Channel (email, social, etc.):

_____

Core Sales Mechanism (DMs, calls, sales page, etc.):

_____

Main Offer They're Guided Into:

_____

THE AI + TOOL STACK

This is the simple, streamlined set of tools that supports everything you build without overwhelming you or adding unnecessary complexity.

Core Tools

- **ChatGPT** — strategy, content, automation, clarity
- **Canva** — graphics, PDFs, brand assets
- **Google Drive or Notion** — organization, documents, planning
- **Stripe** — payments

Email & Nurture

- **MailerLite or ConvertKit** — simple, intuitive, automation-friendly

Sales & Delivery

- **Gumroad, Shopify, or Stan Store** — product hosting, digital downloads
- **Link-in-bio tool** — easy navigation from social platforms

Content Creation & Scheduling

- **CapCut** — short-form video editing
- **Meta & TikTok schedulers** — posting automation
- **Google Calendar** — content cycles and CEO planning

Optional Support Tools

- AI transcription tools
- Pinterest schedulers
- Simple funnel builders if needed later

Your business doesn't require a tech stack, only a steady foundation supported by tools that lighten your load and amplify your voice.

SECTION 8
EMAIL, NURTURE & CLIENT EXPERIENCE

"Prompts to build simple email sequences and unforgettable experiences."

HOW TO USE THESE PROMPTS

1. Choose your main nurture channel (email is recommended).
2. Use prompts to create sequences and client journeys.

PROMPTS

1. "Design a 5-email welcome sequence for new subscribers that:
   – introduces who I am
   – clarifies who I help
   – shares my core beliefs
   – gives quick value
   – softly introduces my core offer."
2. "Write a simple 'content plan' for my weekly or bi-weekly newsletter for the next 12 weeks."
3. "Design a short sales email sequence (5–7 emails) to promote my core offer to warm subscribers."
4. "Map out my ideal client experience from 'yes' to 'finish' for my core offer. Where can I overdeliver in simple, sustainable ways?"
5. "What automations (tagging, reminders, follow-ups) would make my nurture and client delivery smoother without feeling robotic?"
6. "Write a one-page 'Nurture & Experience' section for my business plan that describes how I take care of my people."

SECTION 9
LAUNCH PLAN (FIRST 90 DAYS)

"Prompts to create a no-overwhelm launch strategy for your main offer."

HOW TO USE THESE PROMPTS

You don't need a complicated launch. You need **clarity, timing, and consistency**.

PROMPTS

1. "Create a simple 90-day launch plan for my core offer: pre-launch (warm up), launch (sell), post-launch (nurture + deliver)."
2. "Outline my content for each phase of the launch (awareness, education, urgency, decision)."
3. "Design a launch strategy that fits my energy and platforms: how often I should post, email, and sell—without burning out."
4. "List 10 low-stress launch actions I can take if my energy is low but I still want to move the needle."
5. "Write a one-page 'Launch Strategy' summary for my business plan that explains how I'll roll out my core offer in Year 1."

SECTION 10
12-MONTH ROADMAP, WEEKLY MILESTONES, HABITS & MINDSET

"Prompts to turn your plan into a timeline and you into the woman who executes it."

HOW TO USE THESE PROMPTS

This is where the TikTok prompt you loved comes in.
We're turning it into **your** execution engine.

PROMPTS: 12-MONTH ROADMAP

1. "Break my first year into 4 quarters and map out my focus for each:
   – Q1: Foundation & first cash
   – Q2: Growth & proof
   – Q3: Scale & systems
   – Q4: Optimization & expansion."

2. "Within each quarter, suggest 3–5 major milestones (offers launched, systems built, revenue targets)."

3. "Turn this into a simple 12-month roadmap I can drop straight into my business plan."

PROMPTS: WEEKLY MILESTONES & CEO HABITS

4. "Based on my business model and goals, what should my **weekly focus** be? (Content, sales, delivery, building assets, CEO time, rest.)"

5. "Create a 'Weekly CEO Checklist' for me—5–10 actions that, if done consistently, will move me toward $10K/month and beyond."

6. "What habits and boundaries do I need to adopt to operate like a seven-figure entrepreneur, even before the money arrives?"

7. "What 3 mindset shifts will have the biggest impact on my ability to execute this plan?"

8. "Write a one-page 'Million-Dollar Habits & Mindset' section for my business plan that I can re-read every week."

WORKSHEET: YEAR 1 SNAPSHOT

This worksheet offers you a clear, steady view of your first year in business not through pressure or hustle, but through intention and alignment.

It's designed to help you stay rooted in your bigger vision while still taking grounded, consistent steps week by week. Think of it as your year-at-a-glance: a simple map that keeps you focused on what matters most.

Move through each section slowly and honestly. Let your answers reflect not only your goals, but the kind of woman you are becoming.

YEAR 1 THEME

Choose a single word or phrase that captures the essence of your first year. This theme sets the tone for your decisions, your energy, and your growth. Examples:

- Foundation
- Clarity
- Expansion
- Consistency
- Devotion
- Discipline
- Visibility
- Momentum

Your theme becomes your anchor. Something you can return to whenever you feel pulled in too many directions.

Quarter Focus

Break your year into four clear, spacious chapters. Each quarter should have one core focus that feels achievable and aligned.

Examples:
Q1: build foundations
Q2: launch and refine
Q3: grow and stabilize
Q4: optimize and expand

This keeps your year feeling structured, not overwhelming.
It also helps you make decisions with clarity instead of urgency.

Non-Negotiable Weekly Actions

List the simple, consistent habits that move your business forward every single week. These should be grounded, sustainable actions such as:

- posting content
- emailing your list
- selling intentionally
- fulfilling offers
- CEO time
- rest and recalibration

Think of these as the heartbeat of your business. The rhythm that keeps everything flowing.

Mindset I'm Choosing to Lead From

This section is about the internal landscape you're choosing to cultivate. Write the beliefs, attitudes, and energetic commitments you want to embody this year. Examples:

- I lead with clarity.
- I trust the process.
- I move with intention, not urgency.
- I allow my business to grow in alignment with who I am.
- I am building something real, steady, and meaningful.

This is the mindset that carries you through challenges, decisions, and seasons of growth.

This worksheet brings your entire business plan into focus, grounding your long-term vision in the day-to-day actions that make it real.

YEAR 1 THEME:

_____

Quarter Focus:

- Q1: _____
- Q2: _____
- Q3: _____
- Q4: _____

Non-Negotiable Weekly Actions:

_____

Mindset I'm Choosing to Lead From:

_____

KPIs & MEASUREMENT PLAN

This section is the bridge between intention and reality. It gives you clear, simple markers to track each month without pressure, spreadsheets, or perfectionism.

Monthly KPIs to Track

Visibility & Growth
- follower growth (by platform)
- email list growth
- website traffic (if applicable)

Engagement & Conversion
- number of leads generated
- DM conversations or inquiries
- conversion rate from lead → buyer

Financial Health
- monthly revenue
- recurring revenue
- number of sales by offer
- average order value

Output & Consistency
- posts published
- emails sent
- content batches completed

Quarterly Check-Ins

Each quarter, review:
- which offers performed
- what content resonated
- where your time is going
- what should be simplified
- what needs amplification

Why This Matters

These metrics aren't about pressure. They're about awareness, understanding what's growing, what's resonating, and what's ready to evolve.

This brings intelligence, confidence, and intention to your leadership.

THE MASTER CHEAT CODE PROMPT

THE MILLION-DOLLAR BUSINESS PLAN BUILDER

Use this when you're ready to pull everything together into one AI-generated master plan. Copy + paste this into AI and customize the brackets:

MASTER PROMPT

"I want you to act as my personal business strategist and help me build a digital business that can generate at least $1 million in revenue within the next 12–36 months with zero startup capital, no tech background, and a content-driven, passive-income style.

Use everything I've already uncovered in my AI Empire Builder workbooks:
- Step 1: Wealth & Success Mindset (my identity and money story)
- Step 2: Purpose & Passion (my strengths, purpose, and energy)
- Step 3: Million-Dollar Ideas (my aligned business ideas)
- Step 4: Empire Map (my offers, ecosystem, and brand direction).

Start by asking me the most important questions you need to fully understand:
- my strengths and lived experience
- my personality and nervous system
- my time availability each week
- my preferred business style (content-driven, low-overhead, passive income, no complicated tech)
- my income goals for the next 12 months and 3 years.

Then, based on my answers, build me a customized step-by-step business plan that includes:
- a business model that can launch fast with no capital
- a high-demand offer (or offer suite) that people will actually pay for
- a 12-month monetization and growth roadmap
- a content and marketing plan using only free tools and organic platforms
- a simple lead generation system I can execute without ads
- recommended AI tools and ChatGPT prompts to automate as much work as possible
- a scaling system so I can grow without a big team.

Break my plan into:
- Year 1 focus (foundation, first cash, proof of concept)
- Year 2 focus (scale, systems, recurring revenue)
- Year 3 focus (empire, optional team, seven-figure readiness).

Give me:
- weekly milestones and revenue goals
- a 'minimum viable week' schedule I can stick to even when life is chaotic
- mindset shifts and habits I need to embody to execute like a seven-figure entrepreneur.

Make this plan lean, high-leverage, and ruthlessly effective. I want something so powerful it feels like a cheat code. Build my million-dollar business from the ground up, step-by-step."

CLOSING NOTE

You've now built the foundation of a real business plan. One that reflects your identity, your strengths, and the vision you're stepping into. You've shaped your offers, clarified your message, designed your funnel, and mapped the flow of your first year.

This isn't theory.
This is structure.
This is direction.
This is the beginning of your empire: intentional, aligned, and uniquely yours.

Step 5 anchored the *what* and the *how*. It grounded your ideas into a blueprint you can return to every time you need clarity or focus.

Now, you're ready for something deeper: the *pathway* that turns this plan into revenue, momentum, and your first major financial milestones.

Where Step 5 gave you the map, Step 6 reveals the path.

It shows you:
- the fastest route to $100K
- the clear steps to $250K
- the sustainable roadmap to $1M
- the milestones you'll hit along the way
- the bottlenecks to expect
- the weekly actions that compound
- the daily habits that create inevitability

This next step is where your plan becomes a trajectory, a focused, confident path toward the future you're building.

When you're ready, step forward. Let AI help you chart the millionaire path that aligns with your energy, your values, and the woman you are becoming. Your next chapter begins now.

STEP 6:

The Millionaire Path Prompts

"How to Ask AI for a Year-by-Year Income Trajectory & Action Plan"

This is the moment the fog lifts.

This is where guesses turn into **data**, dreams turn into **timelines**, and your income goals turn into an **actual path** you can follow like a map.

You've already built clarity, ideas, an ecosystem, a business model, and a direction. NOW we plug it into AI like a wealth GPS and say:

"Show me the fastest, most aligned path to my millionaire timeline."

AI becomes your:
- income strategist
- revenue modeler
- pacing architect
- scaling advisor
- year-by-year planner
- milestone forecaster
- bottleneck remover
- accountability mirror

This step gives you **prompts that calculate timelines, monthly revenue pacing, milestone targets, growth phases, income ceilings, content strategy, and scaling steps** all based on who you are and the empire you're building.

This is where your financial destiny becomes visible.

WELCOME

Most women build businesses backwards:

- They try random strategies
- They copy influencers without context
- They work hard but not in the right order
- They scale before stabilizing
- They focus on aesthetics before revenue
- They have goals but no map

Step 6 solves this.

This step gives you the power to say:
- "AI, map my fastest path to $10K months."
- "Show me what my business can realistically earn in Year 1."
- "Calculate the 5-year path to $1M for my exact model."
- "Tell me when my first $100K year is likely and why."
- "Break down my monthly milestones so I know what to execute and when."

You are not guessing anymore.
You are choosing your timeline with clarity and intention.

You're no longer hoping for the breakthrough.
You're engineering it.

HOW TO USE STEP 6

Before every prompt in this step, add: **"Act as my income strategist. Base your answers on Steps 1–5 of The AI Empire Builder (my identity, purpose, strengths, business model, offers, and ecosystem). Give me realistic, grounded timelines AND the simplest path forward."**

Then run 1–3 prompts at a time.

Highlight anything that feels:

- clarifying
- doable
- exciting
- aligned

Cross out anything that feels:

- heavy
- unrealistic
- overly complex
- misaligned

Turn each insight into:

- one decision

- one action

- one milestone

This is how you build your income like a CEO.

THE WEALTH MATH FORMULAS

Feed these directly into AI and it will calculate everything for you.

Formula A — $10K/Month Calculator
"Using my offer suite and price points, calculate every possible combination of sales that consistently equals $10K/month. Show me the easiest pathway."

Formula B — $100K/Year Projection
"Using my offers, show every scenario that results in $100K/year. Include low-ticket, mid-tier, premium, and digital products."

Formula C — The $1M Forecast
"Calculate multiple pathways to $1M annually based on my business model. Include:

- monthly pacing

- conversion rates

- audience size

- content volume

- funnel structure

- revenue distribution across tiers"

Formula D — Traffic → Lead → Sale Funnel Math
"Using realistic conversion rates, calculate:

- how many views I need

- how many leads I need

- how many customers I need
  to hit $10K, $30K, $100K, $250K, and $1M."

This is the stuff NO ONE teaches online.

TEACHING PAGE:
HOW MILLION-DOLLAR BUSINESSES ACTUALLY GROW

There is a pattern in every scalable online business:

YEAR 1 — PROOF & CASH FLOW
One core offer.
One primary platform.
Simple digital products.
$50K–$150K range.

YEAR 2 — SYSTEMS & SCALE
More traffic.
More automation.
Memberships or recurring revenue.
$150K–$350K range.

YEAR 3–5 — EMPIRE MOMENTUM
Hiring support.
Expanding the brand.
Premium programs.
Evergreen funnels.
$350K–$1M+ range.

You grow by phases not pressure.

Step 6 reveals which year YOU hit each tier, based on your model, offers, and energy.

YEAR-BY-YEAR WEALTH ROADMAP

"Your Financial Evolution: The Woman You Become as You Rise"

This is one of the most powerful parts of Step 6, because income does not grow in a straight line. **YOU evolve year by year, and your business evolves with you.** Most women look at their goals and see only numbers. What they *don't* see is:

- the identity shift required
- the skills each year teaches you
- the structural upgrades your business must make
- the emotional resilience you build
- the version of you who becomes capable of holding wealth

This roadmap shows you the *actual progression* of a scalable online business and the evolution of the woman running it. Use this section to understand:

- **what year you're in now**
- **what each year demands**
- **what each year unlocks**
- **what skills each year builds**
- **what identity you are stepping into**

This is not a rigid timeline. This is an *archetypal path*, the pattern nearly all successful creators, coaches, entrepreneurs, and online CEOs move through as they grow to multi-six-figures and beyond. It helps you ask AI for clarity, direction, and strategy from a higher vantage point.

How to Use This Roadmap

Copy and paste this prompt into AI: **"Map my 5-year financial evolution. Base it on my current business model, offers, strengths, lifestyle, and the empire I'm building. Outline what each year looks like for ME including income range, priorities, identity upgrades, and what I must master before moving to the next stage."**

Then read the responses slowly. Highlight anything that feels:

- aligned
- true
- exciting
- clarifying

This roadmap is not about pressure. It's about *context.* It helps you see:
- why you're not "behind"
- why your path may feel slow but is actually perfect
- why certain income levels feel harder before they feel easier
- why each year builds the next
- how your identity, confidence, skills, and capacity transform as your wealth grows

When you understand the **sequence**, the chaos calms. You stop comparing timelines. You stop forcing growth. You start trusting your path. This is where the journey becomes *inevitable.*

THE 5-YEAR FINANCIAL EVOLUTION

Below is the high-level blueprint AI will expand for you. These are the five phases nearly all successful digital entrepreneurs move through and the emotional and strategic upgrades that define each one.

Tell AI to outline each one of the bullet points.

YEAR 1 — Identity + Cash Flow

This year is about clarity, momentum, and your first structural foundations.

You create:
- your first signature product
- your first digital ecosystem
- your first 100 customers
- your first $10K month
- your first set of systems
- your minimum viable brand

Identity shift: You stop *dabbling* and start *building.*

YEAR 2 — Scaling Foundation

This year isn't about doing more, it's about doing what works, better and bigger.

You build:
- evergreen content machine
- recurring revenue streams
- traffic expansion strategy
- your first hiring/outsourcing
- your first cohesive product line

Identity shift: You stop being a **creator** and step into being a **CEO.**

YEAR 3 — Empire Stabilization

This is where you become known.

You establish:
- brand authority
- funnel maturity
- multi-platform growth
- premium tier offer
- the capacity for $300K–$600K per year

Identity shift: You finally feel: "This works. I can scale this. This is who I am."

YEAR 4 — Scale to Wealth

This is the year your brand becomes "bigger than you."

You gain:
- automated funnels
- expanded team support
- PR or visibility breakthroughs
- a fully established $1M pipeline

Identity shift:
You stop chasing opportunity and begin **attracting** it.

YEAR 5 — Legacy Brand

This is where your empire becomes undeniable.

You embody:
- a full, multi-offer ecosystem
- multi-six-figure months
- an automated business structure
- an identity that cannot go back to smallness

Identity shift:
You become the woman who holds wealth without fear.
You become the architect of a legacy, not just a business.

Why This Roadmap Matters

Because Step 6 isn't just about hitting financial milestones. It's about becoming the woman who can *hold* them.

The woman who doesn't burn out.
The woman who leads with clarity.
The woman who trusts her timing.
The woman who builds wealth intentionally, sustainably, and with purpose.

This roadmap gives Step 6 its soul
the evolution of the woman behind the money.

SECTION 1
The Fastest Path to $10K/Month

"Prompts that calculate your simplest, most aligned way to hit consistent $10K months."

This is the first true stability milestone in your business, the moment where your income stops feeling accidental and starts feeling *intentional*. The path to $10K/month isn't mysterious. It isn't luck. It isn't guessing. It's a combination of:

- offer clarity
- aligned pricing
- predictable sales volume
- simple content strategy
- consistent weekly actions
- removing the bottlenecks that keep you stuck

This section teaches you how to ask AI to calculate the *exact* steps required for YOU to hit $10K months in the next 3–6 months based on your strengths, your business model, your energy, and the offers you already have.

This is where AI becomes your revenue strategist. Where guesswork disappears. Where simplicity replaces overwhelm. Where you stop "trying" and start **engineering your income.** When you know your $10K path, everything becomes easier:

- your content becomes clearer
- your sales become simpler
- your offer math becomes obvious
- your confidence skyrockets
- your actions stop feeling random
- your progress becomes measurable
- your timeline collapses

The goal of this section? **To show you the quickest, easiest, most aligned path to stability and momentum.**

How to Use This Section

Before using any of the prompts below, say: **"Analyze my business model, personality, offers, and energy. Create a simple, minimalistic, high-ROI path to $10K/month without burnout or complexity."**

Then:

- Run each prompt individually
- Highlight anything that feels aligned
- Circle the strategy that feels light + doable
- Cross out anything that feels heavy or pressured
- Build your $10K roadmap from the pieces that feel true

This section works best when you:
- give AI your offer suite
- include your pricing
- list how much content you're willing to create
- explain your ideal client
- describe your natural strengths
- tell AI how you work best (fast, slow, bursts, structured, creative, etc.)

The more personal you get, the more accurate the $10K plan becomes. This is not about forcing success, it's about discovering the path of least resistance.

PROMPTS FOR YOUR $10K/MONTH BLUEPRINT

Run each one with the pre-prompt above:

1. "Based on my current offers, skills, and business model, what is my FASTEST path to $10K/month in the next 3–6 months? Show the exact steps."
→ This calculates your personal roadmap.

2. "Calculate how many sales I need of each offer to consistently hit $10K/month."
→ This gives you the revenue math.

3. "Which offer should I lead with to reach $10K/month fastest — and why?"
→ This identifies your fastest-converting offer.

4. "What content strategy would help me hit $10K/month with the least resistance?"
→ This shows you the easiest content that converts.

5. "What are my biggest bottlenecks to $10K months — and how do I remove them?"
→ This diagnoses the invisible blocks slowing you down.

6. "What habits and actions generate 80% of my revenue potential right now?"
→ This gives you the highest-ROI tasks.

7. "Break down the exact weekly tasks that move me toward $10K/month."
→ This creates your precise execution plan.

8. "Design a 90-day path to $10K/month based on my model and energy."
→ This becomes your quarter-long sprint.

Why This Section Matters

Because once you know your personal path to $10K/month:

- your mind calms
- your energy stabilizes
- your confidence grows
- your momentum becomes inevitable
- your business stops feeling chaotic
- your choices become laser-focused
- your income becomes predictable

$10K months are the foundation of everything that comes after:

$30K months
$100K months
$300K months
and eventually —
your million-dollar year.

But it all starts here:
your simplest path to stability, clarity, and consistent cash flow.

SECTION 2
The 12-Month Path to $100K

"Prompts that map your first (or next) six-figure year."

A $100K year is not a mystery. It is math, momentum, and alignment. This section shows you how to use AI to architect your next six-figure year with a plan that feels:

- strategic
- grounded
- emotionally sustainable
- energetically aligned
- and realistic for YOUR life

This is where you stop guessing "what should I do next?" and start engineering a year where every quarter, every month, every week has a purpose. AI will map:

- your revenue trajectory
- your monthly pacing
- seasonal fluctuations
- offer contribution
- your effort-to-income ratio
- the first moves that matter and the moves that can wait

This is clarity. This is direction. This is the blueprint that makes six figures feel like the *floor*, not the ceiling. When you see the year broken into four simple phases, everything feels easier:

- You know exactly what to build
- You know what to promote when
- You know the content that drives growth
- You see your bottlenecks before they block you
- You stop overworking and start executing with intention

This isn't "hustle harder." It's **move smarter.** It's **plan intentionally.** It's **expand sustainably.**

How to Use This Section

Before running the prompts, say: **"AI, analyze my goals, offers, pricing, audience, strengths, and available time. Map the simplest and most sustainable path to $100K in the next 12 months."**
Then run each prompt individually. Let AI:

- calculate the numbers
- break the year into seasons
- show you what actually moves the needle
- reveal where you're holding yourself back
- highlight the easy money already available

Once you get your answers:

- highlight anything that feels exciting
- cross out anything that feels heavy
- keep the actions that feel aligned
- plug the milestones into your calendar
- turn the quarterly plan into weekly steps

The more honest you are with AI, the more accurate your six-figure map becomes.

PROMPTS FOR YOUR SIX-FIGURE YEAR

1. "Map out my 12-month path to $100K based on my business model. Break it into four 90-day phases."
→ Your year, simplified.

2. "Calculate my monthly revenue pacing for a $100K year."
→ Breaks the math into manageable goals.

3. "What needs to happen each quarter to hit $100K this year?"
→ Your quarterly focus points.

4. "Analyze my offer suite and tell me which offers contribute most to $100K."
→ Your highest-ROI offers.

5. "What would make a $100K year feel inevitable?"
→ AI identifies your confidence triggers.

6. "Break down the actions, content, and momentum I need to reach $100K sustainably."
→ Your aligned execution plan.

7. "What milestones indicate I'm on track for $100K?"
→ Your progress checkpoints.

8. "What bottlenecks could block my path to $100K and how do I solve them?"
→ Your obstacle removal.

9. "Create a simple $100K Action Plan with 10 steps."
→ Your year distilled into clarity.

Why This Section Matters

Because the difference between a $40K year and a $100K year is not talent. It is not luck. It is not more hours. It is **clarity and consistency.**

Most people try to build a six-figure year with:
- random content
- random launches
- random offers
- random habits

You're not doing that anymore. You are building a **strategic ecosystem** where everything works together. This section turns your year into a predictable journey not a chaotic gamble.

When you finish Section 2, you will know:
- exactly what you're building
- exactly when to promote it
- exactly how much money is possible
- exactly what to improve
- exactly how to pace yourself

Six figures becomes simple, inevitable, and aligned.

SECTION 3
OFFER-BASED REVENUE FORECASTING
"How Each Offer Contributes to Your Wealth Timeline"

This is where AI calculates how EACH offer contributes to wealth. This is the moment where your business stops being a mystery and becomes **predictable.** Instead of guessing which offer will make you money, AI will calculate:

- where your revenue is truly coming from
- which offers drive fast cash
- which offers scale long-term
- which offers plateau
- which offers become your million-dollar pathway

Most women launch offers without understanding their **earning trajectory.** This step solves that. This section teaches you how to ask AI to analyze each offer like a financial strategist using real math, predictable patterns, and revenue modeling. You'll finally see:

- which offers fuel your first $10K
- which ones build your $100K year
- which ones carry your brand to multi-six-figures
- which offer becomes your "Wealth Engine"
- which offers need refinement before they scale
- which offers are distractions
- which offer becomes your **$1M escalator**

When you understand the financial weight of each offer, you stop treating your business like guesswork and start running it like a **data-driven empire.**

How to Use This Section

Before using any prompt, say: **"Analyze my offers using revenue forecasting, conversion math, and realistic industry averages. Give me grounded, strategic projections, not fluffy optimism."**

Then feed AI your full offer suite:

- the name
- the price
- what it includes
- whether it's low-ticket, mid-tier, signature, or premium
- how often you expect to launch it
- how often it's evergreen
- how much content traffic you currently have

The more detail you give, the more accurate your forecasting becomes.

Next:

- Run 1–2 prompts at a time.
- Highlight what feels aligned.

- Circle the offers that create the **fastest cash.**
- Circle the offers that create the **longest growth.**
- Identify your **Wealth Engine** — the offer that carries you to $100K+.
- Identify your **$1M escalator** — the offer that becomes your empire's cornerstone.

This is how you build a business that grows *intentionally* not randomly.

PROMPTS FOR OFFER-BASED REVENUE FORECASTING

Use these one by one:

1. "Analyze the earning potential of each offer in my suite over 12 months."
AI will calculate income potential based on price × demand × conversions.

2. "Calculate what happens if only my low-ticket products perform well. Then calculate the upside if my core offer converts above average."
This shows your "safety floor" and your "ceiling potential."

3. "Which offer gives me the shortest path to $10K? $30K? $100K?"
This identifies your **fastest cash creator.**

4. "Which offer becomes my $1M escalator?"
This identifies the long-term offer that can scale exponentially.

Why This Matters

Most entrepreneurs:
- overestimate the wrong offers
- underprice the right ones
- scale offer suites that were never scalable
- rely on low-ticket products that drain time
- ignore the offer that could make them rich
- build businesses with no revenue structure

This step corrects all of that.

When you understand how each offer contributes to your wealth timeline, you stop feeling lost and start making CEO-level decisions.

This is the section that turns your entire business from:

"I hope this works" → **"I know exactly what leads me to $10K, $100K, and $1M."**

SECTION 4
AUDIENCE SIZE VS. INCOME

"Exactly How Big Your Audience Needs to Be for Your Wealth Timeline"

This is CRITICAL. This is one of the most misunderstood parts of online business. Most women believe they need:

- a huge following
- viral content
- massive reach
- endless posting

…to hit big revenue milestones.

It's not true.

Your income is not determined by your audience size, It's determined by:

- your offer mix
- your conversion rates
- your pricing
- your content strategy
- your funnel maturity
- your message clarity
- your identity as a leader

This section teaches you how to use AI to calculate the **real numbers** behind your goals:

- How many followers you actually need.
- How many email subscribers.
- How many leads.
- How many customers.
- How many conversions.
- How many monthly views.

Not guesswork. Not influencer fantasy. Actual math. This is where your empire stops running on vibes and starts running on *data*.

How to Use This Section

Before each prompt, say: **"Analyze my audience needs using realistic conversion rates (1–5% for email, .5–3% for social), industry benchmarks, my pricing, my business model, and my content style."**

Then run the prompts one by one.

As you go:

- Highlight the platform with the highest ROI
- Circle the numbers that feel easiest to hit
- Note where your conversions naturally tend to be higher

- Identify which platform becomes your wealth amplifier
- Mark the platforms you can release without losing momentum

This is NOT about pressuring yourself to grow. This is about clarity.

Clarity reduces anxiety.
Clarity reduces overwhelm.
Clarity helps you grow strategically instead of frantically.
Clarity shows you the *easiest* path to wealth based on your strengths and your natural magnetism.

Prompts for Audience Size vs. Income Forecasting

Use all four prompts, they create your complete visibility blueprint.

1. "Calculate how many followers I need on each platform to hit my revenue goals."

AI will factor in:
- conversion rates
- traffic patterns
- platform behavior
- your offer pricing
- your sales cycle

This shows which platforms require the least effort for the greatest return.

2. "How big does my email list need to be for $10K months?"

Email converts 10–20x higher than social. This one prompt alone can collapse YEARS off your timeline.

3. "What if I want a $1M year with a tiny audience? Show the offer mix required."

This is your **high-ticket, boutique, low-volume empire** option. It's how small creators build massive revenue.

4. "What would collapse my need for a large audience entirely?"

AI will show you:
- which offers
- which prices
- which funnels
- which content strategy
- which platforms

…let you scale FAST without needing tens of thousands of followers.

This is the answer to the question every creator secretly asks:

"Can I get rich without going viral?"
(Yes, baby. Very much yes.)

Why This Matters

Because this step removes the biggest lie women are told online:

That they need to be everywhere.
That they need to be everything.
That they need to post constantly.
That they need to go viral.
That they need a massive following to hit big numbers.

Your audience is not your limitation, it's your multiplier. Once you understand how many people you *actually* need…

You stop chasing followers and start building wealth.
You stop burning yourself out and start building systems.
You stop comparing yourself and start owning your lane.

This section gives you the **visibility blueprint** behind your millionaire timeline rooted in clarity, realism, and CEO-level strategy.

SECTION 5
Revenue Ceilings & Income Potential

"Prompts to predict the max earning potential of your offers, model, and audience."

Every offer has a natural revenue ceiling. Every business model has a built-in limit. Every audience size can only support so much. But every entrepreneur has a *much larger* capacity than they realize. This section reveals the truth: where your current income tops out and where your future income multiplies.

Knowing your revenue ceilings is power. It stops you from wasting time on offers that won't scale. It shows you where you're unconsciously holding your income down. And it illuminates what needs to shift to step into real wealth.

When AI analyzes your income potential, it becomes your:
- strategist
- forecaster
- economist
- scale architect
- blind-spot detector

This section tells you:
- which offer can scale alone
- which offer caps your income
- which part of your business bottlenecks your growth
- what your current audience can realistically support
- what would 10x your earning capacity
- what you need to add later for multi-six-figure or million-dollar expansion

This isn't about guessing how much you *think* you can earn. It's about identifying how much you're actually sitting on and what needs to evolve to reach your highest income potential.

How to Use This Section

Before running these prompts, tell AI: **"Evaluate my business model, offers, pricing, audience size, content capacity, and personal energy. Show me my true earning potential and what limitations I need to remove."**

Then:
- Look for patterns in AI's responses
- Highlight the offers with the highest scale potential
- Circle the bottlenecks that feel familiar
- Notice where your own beliefs cap your income
- Let AI identify the structural limits you can't see yourself

This section is not about doing more. It's about **opening more capacity.** Your revenue ceiling is not permanent, it's the version of you you're about to surpass.

PROMPTS FOR REVENUE CEILINGS & INCOME POTENTIAL

1. "Analyze each of my offers and calculate the revenue ceiling of each one."
→ Determines the maximum each offer can generate.

2. "Which offer has the highest potential to scale to $100K/year on its own?"
→ Identifies your most scalable offer.

3. "What parts of my business model cap my income and how do I remove those caps?"
→ Reveals structural + energetic limitations.

4. "What revenue level can my current audience size realistically support?"
→ Gives you a grounded income baseline.

5. "What changes would 10x my income capacity?"
→ Shows your fastest path to exponential growth.

6. "What offers need to be added later to expand my earning ceiling?"
→ Helps you build a multi-tier ecosystem.

7. "Which parts of my business model are the most (and least) scalable?"
→ Clarifies what to keep, improve, or replace.

Why This Section Matters

Because you cannot scale what you cannot see. Most women build businesses with:
- low ceilings
- capped models
- low-ROI offers
- too many time-based services

- too much energy output
- not enough leverage
- and no map for exponential growth

This section fixes that. When you understand your revenue ceilings:
- you know which offer becomes your workhorse
- you know what to improve
- you know where to simplify
- you know where to shift your time
- you know where your million-dollar potential is hiding

And most importantly: You stop building from fear and start scaling from clarity.

SECTION 6
SCALING PATHWAYS (3 Models)

"Choose the millionaire model that matches your energy, your brand, and your destiny."

Every millionaire entrepreneur follows one of three core scaling pathways or a custom hybrid of all three. These pathways determine:
- how you grow
- how you sell
- how you automate
- how you expand
- and what your income *wants* to do naturally

Scaling isn't random. It's patterned. It's predictable. And when you align with the model that fits your energy, your wealth timeline **collapses**. In this section, AI will help you identify which millionaire pathway matches:
- your personality
- your capacity
- your creativity
- your strengths
- your vision
- your lifestyle
- your revenue goals

And most importantly: your **energetic blueprint** as a woman building a digital empire. There is no "one right way." There is only: **your way: amplified.**

Below are the three millionaire scaling models.

146

THE THREE MILLIONAIRE MODELS

These are the pathways every 7-figure brand uses (whether they realize it or not):

4. The Content Empire Model

Traffic → Trust → Digital Products → Recurring → Premium

This is for the creator, the storyteller, the teacher, the vibe-setter. It scales through:
- high-trust content
- evergreen posts that sell for you
- signature digital products
- memberships or recurring offers
- and a premium anchor offer

This model builds influence, authority, and a deep, loyal audience. Perfect for the woman whose presence *is* the brand.

5. The Evergreen Funnel Model

Paid or Organic → Automation → High-Frequency Sales

This is for the strategist, the system-builder, the one who loves structure. It scales through:
- automated funnels
- email sequences
- lead generation
- evergreen webinars
- predictable daily sales

This model creates stability and high recurring revenue with minimal daily output. Perfect for the woman who wants wealth on autopilot.

6. The Multiproduct Digital Store Model

High-volume digital downloads → Bundles → Upsells → Escalators

This is for the builder, the creator, the "digital machine." It scales through:
- high-demand, low-ticket products
- massive catalog growth
- bundles that stack value
- upsells to core offers
- escalators to premium tiers

Perfect for the woman who wants wide reach, diverse income streams, and rapid scaling through volume.

How to Use This Section

Before you run the prompts, say: **"Analyze my goals, offers, personality, strengths, content style, energy levels, and long-term vision. Identify which scaling pathway or hybrid matches me best."**

Then:

- Run the two prompts below
- Compare the AI's reasoning
- Notice which model *feels* right in your body
- Highlight the elements you naturally gravitate toward
- Pay attention to what lights you up vs. what drains you
- Build your empire around the model that supports your nervous system

If two or all three resonate that means you're a hybrid scaler. AI will show you how to blend the pathways into your custom millionaire blueprint.

PROMPTS FOR SCALING PATHWAYS

1. "Which millionaire scaling model fits my energy and brand the best?"
→ AI identifies your primary wealth pathway.

2. "What hybrid model creates the fastest wealth timeline for me?"
→ AI designs your personalized millionaire strategy.

Why This Section Matters

Because scaling is not about doing everything.
It's about committing to the right **pathway** and letting it expand you.

When you know your model:

- your marketing becomes clearer

- your offers make more sense

- your content gets easier

- your income stabilizes

- your growth accelerates

- your decisions simplify

- your timeline collapses

Most women build their businesses in misaligned models and that's why growth feels hard. This section ensures you scale in the way your **soul** prefers, not the way the industry expects.

SECTION 7
The 5-Year Path to $1M+

"Prompts to map the long-term empire timeline: the evolution of your brand, your income, and your identity."

This is where you stop thinking in months and start thinking in **eras.** No more "How do I make money right now?"

Now you are asking:

"Who am I becoming as a millionaire?"

This section maps the five-year transformation from:

Year 1: Income Baseline
→ clarity, cash flow, first systems, first proof of concept

Year 2: Stabilizing
→ consistent revenue, recurring offers, predictable sales

Year 3: Scaling
→ multi-offer ecosystem, brand authority, leveraged growth

Year 4: Expansion
→ PR, teams, visibility, evergreen dominance, premium tiers

Year 5: Empire
→ full ecosystem, multiple revenue streams, wealth identity locked in

Your million-dollar path is not a straight line. It is a **metamorphosis**: financially, creatively, emotionally, and energetically. AI will reveal:
- your revenue ranges each year
- what needs to be built when
- which offers unlock which level
- what roles or automations you'll need
- which identity shifts matter most
- where your personal leadership evolves
- which moves collapse your timeline
- where you can create exponential growth

This is not about pushing harder.
It's about **becoming the woman whose life naturally produces wealth.**

How to Use This Section

Before running the prompts, say: **"AI, analyze my business model, strengths, energy levels, personality, long-term vision, and preferred lifestyle. Map the simplest and most aligned five-year path to $1M+ and beyond."**

Then:
- Run each prompt individually
- Look at the patterns across the responses
- Highlight milestones that feel exciting
- Cross out action items you don't want to carry into your empire
- Notice what Year 5 You is doing and choose to step toward her

This section works best when you:
- have already run your $10K/month plan
- have a sense of your offer suite
- understand your revenue ceilings
- know your ideal scaling model
- can see your future from a place of calm clarity

Let AI guide the strategy, you guide the identity.

PROMPTS FOR YOUR 5-YEAR MILLIONAIRE PATH

1. "Map my 5-year trajectory based on my business model. Show revenue ranges for each year and WHY."
→ The long-term blueprint.

2. "Break down the simplest path to $1M+ in 5 years."
→ The clean, aligned route.

3. "What needs to happen in each year to reach $1M+?"
→ The milestones, the growth, the shifts.

4. "What does my business look like at each income tier: $100K, $250K, $500K, $1M?"
→ The evolution of your ecosystem.

5. "What roles or automations do I need to hire or implement year-by-year?"
→ Your team + systems roadmap.

6. "What would make my $1M timeline collapse faster (without burnout)?"
→ The acceleration levers.

7. "Create the '5-Year CEO Plan' based on my strengths, energy, and long-term vision."
→ Your leadership evolution.

Why This Section Matters

Because millionaires are not built from frantic action, they are built from **long-term clarity.**

When you know your 5-year path:
- you stop self-sabotaging
- you stop rushing
- you stop comparing your timeline to anyone else's
- you stop trying to build Year 5 results with Year 1 energy

And instead:

- You pace your growth
- You make decisions like a CEO
- You choose sustainability over speed
- You build offers that last
- You walk into wealth with strategy, not hope

This section gives you the greatest gift in entrepreneurship: **a long-term vision that feels inevitable.**

SECTION 8
Timeline Collapse

"Where your 5-year path compresses into 2 years... or 1. This is the frequency of acceleration, inevitability, and quantum scaling."

Most people build wealth on a linear timeline. You are not "most people."

Timeline Collapse is the art and science of compressing your millionaire journey:

5 years → 2 years → 12 months → 6 months.

This is not about working harder. Or hustling more hours. Or burning yourself out for speed. Timeline collapse happens when:
- identity shifts faster than circumstances
- decisions sharpen
- bottlenecks dissolve
- systems do the heavy lifting
- future you becomes your operating system
- offers align with your effortless strengths
- automation replaces manual effort
- you stop delaying wealth with unnecessary steps

This is the section that takes your millionaire timeline from: **"Someday..."** → **"Now."**

AI will show you:
- what needs to be true for rapid acceleration
- what you must drop to move faster
- what to automate *immediately*
- what offer mix collapses time
- which actions create disproportionate results
- the difference between a 5-year plan and a 6-month surge
- how to make your timeline inevitable, not aspirational

This is where you ask for a plan that bends reality in your direction.

How to Use This Section

Before you run these prompts, say: **"AI, evaluate my current identity, habits, offers, systems, audience size, energy, and strengths. Show me the fastest path to collapsing my millionaire timeline without burnout."**

Then:

- Run each collapse-level prompt
- Highlight the "quantum moves" that feel powerful
- Pay attention to what creates the biggest jumps
- Remove anything that slows your timeline
- Prioritize automation, simplification, and leverage
- Ignore anything that feels like hustle, pressure, or force
- Choose collapse from clarity, not urgency

This section shows you the difference between:

- a **5-year millionaire**
- a **2-year millionaire**
- a **12-month millionaire**
- a **6-month acceleration anomaly**

You'll feel the version of you that moves faster without working harder.

TIMELINE COLLAPSE PROMPTS

1. "If I wanted to collapse my 5-year millionaire path into 24 months, what would have to be true?"

→ AI identifies your 2-year acceleration levers.

2. "What would collapse it into 12 months?"

→ The year-long quantum expansion.

3. "What would collapse it into 6 months?"

→ The fastest timeline possible without burnout.

4. "What are the non-negotiables for a 7-figure acceleration path?"

→ The behaviors + systems required to stabilize rapid growth.

5. "What must I automate immediately to collapse time?"

→ Your instant timeline-collapsing action plan.

Why This Section Matters

Because wealthy women do not wait for the timeline they're given. they choose the timeline they lead. Timeline collapse is:

- mindset
- identity
- energy
- strategy
- systems
- math
- and self-permission

It's where you stop building a business and start **building inevitability.** This is the level that makes Step 6 feel elite. Not light. Not optional. Not scattered. This is the moment where your empire becomes a living timeline you step into not chase.

SECTION 9
Scaling Plan Prompts

"Prompts that show you how to grow without burnout. Scaling with clarity, ease, and energetic alignment."

Scaling is not about doing more. It is not about forcing growth. It is not about adding chaos to an already-full life. Sustainable scaling is:

- **intentional**
- **minimalistic**
- **focused**
- **structural**
- **energetically supportive**

And aligned with the woman you are becoming not the woman you used to be. This section teaches you how to use AI to design a scaling plan that feels:

- calm
- organized
- predictable
- refined
- structured
- regenerative
- and deeply aligned with your nervous system

AI will reveal:

- which offer becomes your scalable signature
- what systems need to be built first
- which tasks must be automated
- what content can run on evergreen
- where your biggest energy leaks are
- what you must **stop** doing to expand
- how to move from "doing everything" to "doing what moves the needle"

Scaling is not about effort. It's about elegance. This is where your business evolves from "creator" to **CEO**.

How to Use This Section

Before running the prompts, tell AI: **"Analyze my business model, personality, strengths, energy, capacity, and long-term goals. Create a scaling plan that grows my income without increasing my workload."**

Then:

- Run each prompt individually
- Highlight the parts that feel like pure relief
- Circle the actions that create the biggest impact
- Note the tasks that drain you. These are your stop-doing list
- Identify the systems that can replace 80% of your manual output
- Lean heavily into automation, evergreen, and leverage

Scaling happens when you build:
- systems that do the work
- content that sells for you
- offers that deliver without draining you
- habits that keep you in your power
- boundaries that protect your energy
- support that multiplies your efforts

This is where your business begins to breathe on its own.

SCALING PLAN PROMPTS

1. "What is my most aligned scaling plan based on my strengths and energy?"
→ Your personalized millionaire pathway.

2. "What offer becomes my scalable signature?"
→ The offer that carries your empire forward.

3. "What needs to be automated first in my business?"
→ Your highest-leverage systems.

4. "What content should become evergreen?"
→ Your long-term sales drivers.

5. "What systems do I need to scale sustainably?"
→ Your infrastructure blueprint.

6. "What do I need to STOP doing to scale faster?"
→ Your liberation list — the tasks you outgrow.

Why This Section Matters

Because most women fail to scale not from lack of effort, but from **too much** effort in the wrong direction. When you know your scaling plan:
- your actions simplify
- your path becomes clear
- your systems carry more weight than your body
- your offers work harder than you do
- your content sells while you sleep
- your business stops depending on your energy
- your revenue stabilizes
- your growth accelerates

This is the moment where your business stops being a hustle and becomes a **machine.** Scaling without burnout isn't just possible, it's the only way to build the empire you're meant for.

SECTION 10
Bottlenecks, Breakpoints, & Burnout Points

"The shadow side of scaling. The places where most creators crack, and how to rise instead of break."

Every business has breaking points. Every income tier has its own pressure. Every scaling leap exposes the patterns you still need to clean up. You don't hit a wall because you're unmotivated. You hit a wall because your **systems, identity, or energetic capacity** are not built for the level you're trying to hold.

This section is where AI helps you see:
- what breaks at each income tier
- what emotional patterns you will outgrow
- what operational gaps will stop you
- what systems must be built BEFORE you scale
- what pressure points appear as you rise
- where burnout tends to creep in
- how to reinforce your foundations BEFORE they crack
- how to expand without collapsing

This is not the "cute" part of scaling. This is the **truth-telling** part, the part no one teaches. When you understand your bottlenecks:
- scaling becomes smoother
- income becomes steadier
- launches feel lighter
- your body feels safer
- your nervous system relaxes
- your leadership expands
- your empire becomes sustainable

You stop sabotaging. You stop shrinking. You stop hitting the same wall. You rise into your next level with eyes wide open.

How to Use This Section

Before running the prompts, tell AI: **"Analyze my business model, habits, identity patterns, emotional triggers, systems, and offers. Show me the exact bottlenecks that will appear at each income tier — and how to remove them BEFORE I scale."**

Then:
- Run each prompt
- Highlight the patterns you already recognize
- Circle the emotional triggers that feel familiar
- Note where your current systems are insufficient
- Identify what needs to be built BEFORE you hit the next tier
- Ask AI for solutions that feel supportive, not stressful

This section works best when you're brutally honest:

- about what drains you
- about what overwhelms you
- about what you avoid
- about what breaks your momentum
- about what sabotages your confidence

Your empire will only grow as high as the emotional and structural foundations you build here.

BOTTLENECK & BREAKPOINT PROMPTS

1. "What breaks at $10K/month for most creators — and how do I prevent it?"
→ Reveals early-stage bottlenecks (capacity, time, structure).

2. "What breaks at $30K/month?"
→ Identifies the mid-tier pressure points (offer delivery, boundaries, systems).

3. "What breaks at $100K months?"
→ Shows the high-level breakpoints (team, automation, leadership, identity).

4. "What emotional patterns will I outgrow at each tier?"
→ Maps your identity evolution.

5. "What systems MUST be in place before scaling?"
→ Your structural protection against burnout.

Why This Section Matters

Because income does not break you.
Lack of structure does. Lack of boundaries does.
Outdated identity patterns do.
Scaling too fast without support does.
Trying to hold new levels with old habits does.

When you understand your breakpoints:

- your growth becomes softer
- your income becomes sustainable
- your body feels safer to receive
- your leadership deepens
- your confidence expands
- your timeline accelerates
- your business stops leaking energy
- you stop burning out at the same threshold

Most women never scale because they don't know what's breaking them. You will. This is the section that makes your millionaire path **solid.** This is the section that makes your empire **indestructible.**

SECTION 11
Monthly, Weekly & Daily Execution Prompts

"Because millionaire milestones are built through micro-momentum. The small actions that compound into a legacy."

A million-dollar business is not created by one big moment. It is created through **micro-momentum**:
- monthly clarity
- weekly focus
- daily high-leverage actions

This section is where your income stops being a concept and becomes a **routine.** Millionaire women don't guess what to do each day. They don't rely on motivation. They don't operate from chaos. They operate from:
- structure
- repetition
- predictable habits
- aligned workflows
- revenue-driven actions

This is the section that builds your *operating system*, the rhythm that makes your income inevitable.

AI will help you:
- break your goals down into doable monthly targets
- convert those targets into weekly priorities
- identify the daily actions that actually make money
- eliminate the tasks that drain your time
- create a 7-day acceleration plan anytime you want to leap forward

This is not "discipline."
This is **design.**
Your future wealth depends on the routines you install here.

How to Use This Section

Before running the prompts, say: **"AI, analyze my goals, schedule, strengths, energy, productivity style, and available time. Create an execution plan that moves me toward millionaire outcomes without burnout."**

Then:
- Run each prompt
- Highlight the steps that feel energizing
- Circle anything that feels simple and doable
- Cross out anything that feels heavy or draining
- Add your monthly and weekly rhythm into a calendar
- Keep your daily actions to 1–3 high-leverage tasks (max)

The key is to ask AI for **simplicity**, not perfection. Your daily actions should feel light, repeatable, and aligned. Things you can commit to long-term.

This section becomes your:
- momentum engine
- time-management system
- revenue-generation workflow
- alignment check
- productivity compass

MONTHLY, WEEKLY & DAILY EXECUTION PROMPTS

1. "Break down my goals into monthly income targets and weekly execution steps."
→ Turns the big picture into a clear, structured plan.

2. "What should my weekly workflow look like to hit my revenue goals?"
→ Your income-aligned weekly rhythm.

3. "What are my 'high-leverage' daily actions (the ones that make me money)?"
→ Your money-making habits.

4. "What tasks should I permanently eliminate?"
→ Your stop-doing list — your freedom list.

5. "What should I do in the next 7 days to accelerate my income timeline?"
→ Your short-term sprint plan.

Why This Section Matters

Because millionaire timelines are not built through chaos. They're built through **compounding clarity.**

When your month is structured, you stop drifting.
When your week is focused, you stop spinning.
When your days contain high-leverage actions, you stop wasting time.

This section transforms you from:
- "I hope I'm doing enough"
  to
- **"I know exactly what moves my income."**

It eliminates overwhelm. It removes guesswork. It installs mastery.

This is the moment where your identity shifts from entrepreneur to **inevitable millionaire.**

SECTION 12
The Millionaire Cost Map

"Most people plan income. Millionaires plan costs. This is where you learn how wealth is actually built."

Income is only half of the equation. The women who reach millionaire status fastest are not the ones who make the most money, they are the ones who **manage their costs with precision.**

This section teaches you what no coach tells you:
- how your expenses evolve at each income tier
- what investments accelerate your timeline
- what drains your runway
- what to outsource (and when)
- what to avoid buying completely
- how to stay lean without staying limited
- how to build an empire without reckless spending
- how to make every dollar work harder than you do

This is the difference between:

"I'm growing a business"
and
"I'm building a scalable asset that produces wealth."

AI will show you:
- where your money should go
- where it should NOT go
- what costs are essential vs. optional
- what investments collapse your timeline
- what becomes your financial bottleneck
- how to run your business like a CEO, not a creator

This section turns you into the kind of woman who doesn't fear numbers, she **uses them to multiply her future.**

How to Use This Section

Before running the prompts, say: **"AI, analyze my business model, goals, financial situation, offers, systems, and income tiers. Map my smartest investments, leanest cost structure, and highest-ROI decisions at every stage of growth."**

Then:
- Run each prompt
- Highlight the investments that feel aligned
- Circle the expenses that drain you (remove them)
- Identify what to outsource and when
- Build your "lean path" to millionaire status
- Ask yourself: *"Does this cost accelerate wealth, or delay it?"*

159

This section becomes your:
- financial strategy
- investment compass
- runway protector
- wealth amplifier
- CEO roadmap

It prevents the two biggest wealth killers:
1. **Investing too early** (burnout + drained runway)
2. **Investing too late** (stagnation + bottlenecks)

This is where you learn to scale **intelligently**.

MILLIONAIRE COST MAP PROMPTS

1. "What investments accelerate my timeline vs. drain my runway?"
→ Your acceleration levers vs. your financial liabilities.

2. "What should I spend on at each income tier:
• **$0–$10K**
• **$10K–$30K**
• **$30K–$100K**
• **$100K–$300K**
• **$300K–$1M ?"**
→ Your financial blueprint, tier by tier.

3. "What should I *not* spend money on at each tier?"
→ Prevents premature, wasteful, or low-ROI spending.

4. "What will I need to outsource to scale sustainably?"
→ Your hiring + delegation roadmap.

5. "What is the leanest path to my financial goals with the highest ROI?"
→ Your cash-efficient millionaire plan.

Why This Section Matters

Because most creators fail to scale due to **financial misalignment**, not lack of effort. They:
- spend too soon
- spend too much
- spend on the wrong things
- don't know what matters at each tier
- outsource too early or too late
- invest emotionally instead of strategically
- try to scale with no operational runway

Millionaires think differently: They conserve. They invest intentionally. They optimize. They protect their energy *and* their money. They build lean and expand smart.

Your income timeline accelerates when your **costs** are leveraged, aligned, and optimized. This section turns your business into a financially intelligent empire not a chaotic passion project.

SECTION 13
Execution Maps

"Where strategy becomes motion. Where momentum becomes inevitable. Where your empire begins to run on rhythm instead of force."

This is the final and most important section of Step 6. Because all the millionaire clarity in the world means nothing if you don't have a map that turns it into movement.

Execution Maps take your:

- 5-year vision
- 12-month roadmap
- revenue ceilings
- scaling plan
- bottleneck awareness
- cost strategy

…and condense them into:

30 days
90 days
1 week
1 day.

This is where your big blueprint becomes your *next step.* Where overwhelm dissolves. Where you stop feeling behind and start feeling unstoppable. Execution Maps are the bridge between:

Who you are today → Who you are becoming.
Your current results → Your millionaire identity.

When you ask AI to build these maps, it will show you:

- the fastest way to create cash in the next 30 days
- how to generate momentum that compounds for 90 days
- what you must do weekly to stay on the millionaire path
- the daily actions that guarantee you don't drift
- the habits that keep you aligned
- the non-negotiables that shape your future wealth

This is how millionaires are made through consistent, aligned, predictable execution.

Not hustle. Not chaos. Not pressure. **RHYTHM. REPETITION. RESOLVE.**

How to Use This Section

Before running these prompts, tell AI: **"Analyze my goals, energy, schedule, capacity, revenue targets, and identity work. Create execution maps that simplify my path, amplify my momentum, and keep me aligned with my millionaire timeline."**

Then:
- Run the 30-day plan
- Run the 90-day plan
- Run the weekly rhythm
- Run the daily non-negotiables

After that:
- highlight anything that feels expansive
- circle the tasks that feel naturally aligned
- cross out anything that feels heavy or unrealistic
- add the weekly plan to your calendar
- add the daily non-negotiables to your morning routine
- build your next 30 and 90 days from these maps

The key here is **simplicity.** The plan should feel doable, exciting, aligned not burdensome. Execution Maps are meant to give your business a heartbeat.

EXECUTION MAP PROMPTS

1. "Create a 30-day cash acceleration plan for my business model."
→ Your short-term revenue surge.

2. "Create a 90-day momentum plan."
→ Your quarterly expansion blueprint.

3. "What must I do weekly to stay on pace for my income timeline?"
→ Your millionaire weekly rhythm.

4. "What are my daily non-negotiables as a future millionaire?"
→ Your identity-driven daily habits.

Why This Section Matters

Because millionaires are not built on inspiration, they're built on **consistent execution.**
When you have execution maps:
- you always know what to do next
- you don't lose momentum
- you don't drift into confusion
- you don't sabotage yourself with over-planning
- you avoid burnout because everything is intentional
- you move in alignment with your future, not your fears

Your business stops being reactive and becomes **inevitable.**
Your progress stops feeling sporadic and becomes **predictable.**
Your success stops depending on motivation and becomes **structural.**

This is the moment where Step 6 locks into your body.
This is where you become the woman whose actions match her vision.
This is where your empire starts breathing on its own.

WORKSHEET 1
Millionaire Path Snapshot

"Your entire income timeline distilled into one page: clarity you can see, hold, and act on."

This worksheet is where everything in Step 6 comes together. All the prompts, all the calculations, all the scaling plans, all the timelines, all the revenue maps condensed into the clearest summary of your millionaire path. The goal of this worksheet is simple: **to give you a one-page snapshot of your next five years, your next twelve months, and your next identity.** This is the page you return to:

- when you feel lost
- when you lose momentum
- when you forget the big picture
- when you start overthinking
- when you need grounding
- when you make decisions
- when you choose your next step

Your Millionaire Path Snapshot becomes the compass for:

- your content
- your offers
- your systems
- your investments
- your priorities
- your daily actions
- your scaling decisions

This page is the **heartbeat of your empire.**

How to Use This Worksheet

Before filling it out, complete all relevant prompts in Step 6:

- Your $10K/month breakdown
- Your 12-month $100K plan
- Your offer revenue ceilings
- Your 5-year millionaire trajectory
- Your bottleneck + cost map
- Your scaling model
- Your execution maps

Then:

1. **Copy the clearest, strongest answers into this worksheet.**
   Don't overthink it. Go with what feels aligned and true.
2. **Write in full sentences, not fragments.**
   This helps your mind commit to the identity and strategy.
3. **Be honest about your bottlenecks.**
   Clarity here collapses timelines.
4. **Let your identity decision be bold.**
   This is the new you. The woman who runs the empire.

5. **Print it, screenshot it, or save it somewhere sacred.**
   This becomes your recalibration tool.
6. **Review it weekly.**
   Micro-momentum comes from remembering your direction.

This worksheet isn't about getting it "perfect." It's about getting it **true.** Your millionaire path is already in motion. This page simply makes it visible.

Millionaire Path Snapshot Fields

These are the pieces of clarity you are consolidating:

My Fastest Path to $10K/Month:

_____

My 12-Month Revenue Goal:

_____

Monthly Revenue Targets:

_____

My Highest-ROI Offers:

_____

My Income Bottlenecks:

_____

My Scaling Plan (Years 2–5):

_____

My Millionaire Identity Decision:

_____

_____

Why This Worksheet Matters

Because million-dollar businesses aren't built from confusion, they're built from *clarity you can hold in your hands.* When you finish this worksheet, you will have:

- your entire income plan on one page
- your next year mapped
- your next five years understood
- your bottlenecks exposed
- your offers prioritized
- your direction locked in
- your identity upgraded

This page becomes your anchor, your North Star, and the structure that keeps your empire on course.

WORKSHEET 2
THE $10K MONTH CALCULATOR
"Your First Stability Milestone: simplified, clarified, and mapped."

This worksheet is where your business becomes predictable. $10K/month is not a mystery. It is not a miracle. It is **math + alignment + consistency.** This page breaks down every possible path to consistent $10K months based on:

- your current offers
- your price points
- the number of sales required
- the path of least resistance
- the path of highest scalability
- the weekly habits that actually move the needle
- what you must stop doing to make space for real growth

This worksheet turns "I want $10K months" into: **Here's exactly how to get there.**

How to Use This Worksheet

Start this worksheet **after** completing the prompts in:

- Section 1: Fastest Path to $10K/Month
- Section 5: Revenue Ceilings
- Section 9: Scaling Plan
- Section 10: Bottlenecks & Breakpoints
- Section 11: Monthly/Weekly/Daily Execution

These sections give you the insight you need to fill this page with accuracy and clarity.

Then:

1. **List every offer you currently have.**
   Don't list future ideas. Stick to what exists.
2. **Fill in realistic price points.**
   If you want to test a higher price, include it in your notes.
3. **Use AI to calculate all possible combinations.**
   You want at least 3–6 different paths to $10K/month. Some will be easy. Some will be scalable. Some will be both.
4. **Choose the path that feels aligned.**
   Not the "fanciest," not the "hardest," not the "trendiest." The one that feels like a YES in your body.
5. **Identify the weekly actions that actually matter.**
   This becomes your rhythm. Your income engine.
6. **Eliminate what doesn't move you forward.**
   This is the part no one does, but this is what collapses your timeline.

This worksheet gives you emotional permission to simplify and strategic permission to scale. This becomes your $10K blueprint.

THE $10K MONTH CALCULATOR

1. My Current Offers + Price Points

List every offer you have right now. (No future ideas.)

Offer: _____ Price: _____
Offer: _____ Price: _____
Offer: _____ Price: _____
Offer: _____ Price: _____

2. How Many Sales Do I Need for $10K?

Fill in multiple combinations. Use AI to calculate the math.

Offer Price Monthly Sales Needed Notes

3. Easiest Path to $10K/Month

(What feels aligned + doable?)

4. Most Scalable Path to $10K/Month

(Which path grows WITHOUT adding more hours?)

5. What Must I Focus On Weekly to Hit $10K?

(List 3–5 non-negotiables.)

1. _____
2. _____
3. _____
4. _____
5. _____

6. What to Eliminate

(The 80% that doesn't move you forward)

_____

_____

_____

_____

Why This Worksheet Matters

Because $10K months are the foundation of every milestone that follows:

- $30K months
- $100K months
- $300K months
- $1M years

If you can hit $10K once, you can hit it consistently. And once you can hit it consistently, you can scale it predictably.

This worksheet gives you:

- clarity
- direction
- math
- alignment
- simplicity
- momentum

This is the page that turns your dream of stability into a **repeatable system**.

WORKSHEET 3
THE $100K YEAR MAP

"Your First Six-Figure Year in Black & White: simple, structured, and achievable."

This worksheet translates your six-figure vision into a clear, measurable plan. A $100K year becomes real the moment you break it down into:

- monthly pacing
- weekly numbers
- quarterly milestones
- offer contribution
- consistent habits

Most people dream about six figures. This worksheet makes it **mathematically inevitable.** It removes guesswork. It dissolves overwhelm. It shows you exactly what needs to happen and when. This is your map for:

- clarity
- consistency
- direction
- execution
- momentum

When you finish this worksheet, you will know:

- how much money you need to make each month
- what each quarter is designed to build
- which offers drive the bulk of your year
- what you must do consistently to stay on track
- how to pace yourself so you don't burn out
- where your energy should go (and where it shouldn't)

This worksheet becomes your **anchor** for the entire year.

How to Use This Worksheet

Before filling it out, complete:

- Section 2 — The 12-Month Path to $100K
- Section 5 — Revenue Ceilings & Offer Contribution
- Section 11 — Monthly/Weekly/Daily Execution

These sections give you the clarity you need to make accurate decisions below.

Then:

1. **Start with the math.**
   Break $100K into monthly and weekly numbers.
   (Numbers calm the nervous system and create precision.)
2. **Define each quarter's focus.**
   Think strategically:
   Q1: Foundation
   Q2: Momentum
   Q3: Expansion
   Q4: Optimization + Visibility

3. **Identify your top revenue-driving offers.**
   Usually 1–3 offers produce 80% of your income.
4. **List your monthly actions.**
   These should be simple, repeatable, revenue-focused habits.
5. **Write what feels aligned, not forced.**
   The $100K path should feel energizing — not heavy.

Review this worksheet every month to recalibrate your year.

THE $100K YEAR MAP

1. Your $100K Breakdown

$100,000 \div 12$ months = \$_____ per month
$100,000 \div 52$ weeks = \$_____ per week

2. Quarterly Milestones (Q1–Q4)

Q1 (Months 1–3)
Focus: _____
Target Revenue: _____

Q2 (Months 4–6)
Focus: _____
Target Revenue: _____

Q3 (Months 7–9)
Focus: _____
Target Revenue: _____

Q4 (Months 10–12)
Focus: _____
Target Revenue: _____

3. What Offers Create the Bulk of My $100K?

(Write the 1–3 most profitable or scalable ones.)

4. What Needs to Happen Monthly?

(List key actions, habits, and marketing behaviors.)

_____

_____

_____

_____

_____

Why This Worksheet Matters

A $100K year doesn't happen by accident.
It happens through:
- clarity
- pacing
- consistency
- strategic effort
- aligned offers
- simplified execution

This worksheet turns your desire for six figures into a **trackable plan**. One that stays grounded, aligned, and fully within your control.

It gives you:
- the numbers
- the structure
- the rhythm
- the confidence

…and the roadmap to hold your first (or next) six-figure year with ease.

WORKSHEET 4
THE OFFER INCOME FORECAST SHEET

"Map how each offer contributes to your wealth timeline. Clarity that compounds."

Every offer you create fits somewhere in your long-term wealth ecosystem. Some are quick wins. Some are slow burners. Some are leverage points. Some are invisible bottlenecks. And some become your **wealth engine**, the offer that carries your entire empire.

This worksheet shows you:
- how each offer performs
- how much revenue each one can realistically produce
- where your audience is naturally buying
- which price points make sense
- which offers are dead weight
- which ones scale the easiest
- which ones deserve more visibility, refinement, or automation

This worksheet lets you step into the role of **CEO**, not creator. It teaches you to look at your offers as assets, not ideas. Use this anytime you:
- add a new offer
- change your pricing
- update your funnel
- shift your brand direction
- want to stabilize your income
- want to expand your ecosystem
- want to identify what to scale next

This worksheet becomes your offer-forecasting dashboard. The place where your empire's revenue potential becomes undeniable.

How to Use This Worksheet

Before filling it out, complete the prompts in:
- Offer-Based Revenue Forecasting
- Revenue Ceilings
- Scaling Pathways
- Bottlenecks & Breakpoints
- The Millionaire Cost Map

These sections give you the clarity you need to forecast your offers accurately.

Then:
1. **List up to 10 offers.** Include all price points: low-ticket, mid-tier, premium, recurring, bundles.
2. **Estimate monthly sales.** This is not about perfection. it's about alignment and prediction. Use AI if you want numbers based on audience size, traffic, or conversion rates.
3. **Calculate your total predicted monthly revenue.** Add the right-hand column to see how your offer suite performs together.

4. **Identify your wealth engine.** This is the offer that:
   - ✔ feels the easiest
   - ✔ converts the most
   - ✔ requires the least energy
   - ✔ produces the highest ROI

   This is usually the offer you scale first.
5. **Identify offers that need refinement.** These might need:
   - ✔ better marketing
   - ✔ clearer messaging
   - ✔ price adjustment
   - ✔ automation
   - ✔ updated delivery
   - ✔ improved positioning
6. **Use this worksheet monthly or quarterly.** As your business grows, your wealth engine may evolve. Track it.

This worksheet teaches you to build an empire like a strategist, not a guesser.

THE OFFER INCOME FORECAST SHEET

1. Your Offers

(List up to 10.)

1. _____
2. _____
3. _____
4. _____
5. _____
6. _____
7. _____
8. _____
9. _____
10. _____

2. Estimated Monthly Sales

Fill in what feels aligned or let AI calculate based on your audience.

Offer Price Est. Monthly Sales Monthly Revenue

3. My Total Predicted Monthly Revenue

(Total of the right-hand column.)

$_____

4. Which Offer Is My Wealth Engine?

(Your highest ROI with the least effort.)

5. Which Offer Needs Refinement, Visibility, or Support?

Why This Worksheet Matters

Because wealth does not come from "having a lot of offers." It comes from **knowing which offers create wealth.** This worksheet gives you:

- precision
- clarity
- focus
- strategy
- direction
- confidence

It turns your offer suite into a **scalable ecosystem** instead of a pile of disconnected ideas.

This is how millionaires plan their income with data, alignment, and intentional strategy.

WORKSHEET 5
THE SCALING LADDER MAP
"Your Ascension Path: $0 → $10K → $30K → $100K → $300K → $1M"

See exactly where you are. See exactly what the next level requires. Scaling isn't random. It's sequential. It's patterned. It's predictable. Every income tier has its own:

- identity
- bottlenecks
- systems
- visibility needs
- offer requirements
- emotional upgrades

This worksheet gives you a **ladder**: a clean, simple snapshot of your income evolution, from $0 to your first million-dollar year. Use this anytime you feel:

- stuck
- unclear
- overwhelmed
- unsure why your income isn't rising
- confused about what to build next
- lost between too many plans

This ladder shows you:

- where you are now
- what you've already mastered
- what your next tier requires
- what you're missing
- what needs to be built
- what needs to be removed
- what identity you must step into

It gives you a **zoomed-out map** of your business trajectory without guesswork, chaos, or forced hustle.

How to Use This Worksheet
Before filling it out, complete the prompts in:

- Fastest Path to $10K
- The 12-Month $100K Plan
- Scaling Pathways
- Bottlenecks & Breakpoints
- Revenue Ceilings
- Timeline Collapse
- Execution Maps

These sections give you the clarity you need to accurately identify your tier and next steps.

Then:

1. **Identify the tier you're currently in.** Be honest. Not where you *wish* you were, but where your *income* consistently sits.
2. **Read the focus for your tier.** This is your primary energetic and strategic mission.
3. **Check the boxes that are already complete.** Celebrate what you've mastered. This matters.
4. **Find the one missing piece.** This is the gold. The bottleneck. The block between you and your next income tier.
5. **Use AI to help you build a plan for your missing piece.** Whatever isn't checked becomes your next leap.
6. **Repeat quarterly.** As you scale, your missing pieces evolve, update this map as you ascend.

This worksheet becomes your **quarterly recalibration tool** and your fastest path through each level.

THE SCALING LADDER MAP — WORKSHEET

TIER 1 — $0–$10K/month

Focus: Cash flow + visibility + simplest offer.

To Move to $10K, I Must:
☐ Sell 1 signature offer consistently
☐ Build 1 lead-gen platform
☐ Launch 1 digital product
☐ Stay in one niche

My Missing Piece:

_____

_____

TIER 2 — $10K–$30K/month

Focus: Repeatability + product ecosystem.

To Move to $30K, I Must:
☐ Add recurring revenue
☐ Improve conversions
☐ Increase traffic
☐ Build simple systems

My Missing Piece:

_____

_____

TIER 3 — $30K–$100K/month

Focus: Scaling + automation.

To Move to $100K, I Must:
☐ Automate sales
☐ Add premium tier
☐ Increase audience reach
☐ Expand visibility channels

My Missing Piece:

_____

_____

TIER 4 — $100K–$300K+/month

Focus: Empire-building + team support.

To Move to $300K+, I Must:
☐ Hire support
☐ Create evergreen funnels
☐ Build an omnipresence strategy
☐ Protect energy + creative cycles

My Missing Piece:

_____

_____

Why This Worksheet Matters

Because scaling is not a mystery, it's a sequence. When you know the tier you're in:
- your path becomes obvious
- your decisions get easier
- your actions become more aligned
- your strategy stops jumping around
- your income stabilizes
- your growth accelerates
- your overwhelm dissolves

You move from:
"Why isn't this working?" to "Oh, I'm just missing one piece."

This worksheet gives you the clarity to ascend. Level by level, tier by tier, all the way to your million-dollar year.

WORKSHEET 6
THE BOTTLENECK DIAGNOSIS MAP
"The ACID Test: Awareness, Capacity, Identity, Delivery"

Every plateau has a cause. Every income ceiling has a root. And every stalled creator is stuck in one of the four ACID bottlenecks:

A — Awareness (people don't know you exist)
C — Capacity (you don't have the time or support to scale)
I — Identity (your self-concept can't match the level you're trying to earn at)
D — Delivery (your offer suite or systems can't handle more revenue)

This worksheet reveals **exactly where your growth is leaking**, and which correction instantly accelerates your income timeline. If you don't know what your bottleneck is, you'll prescribe the wrong solution. Posting more when you need systems, lowering prices when you should raise them, adding offers when you should simplify, or working harder when your brand actually just needs visibility. This worksheet gives you clarity, precision, and direction.

HOW TO USE THIS WORKSHEET

1. **Read the four bottleneck categories** (Awareness, Capacity, Identity, Delivery).
2. **Check the symptoms that feel true** — don't judge, don't overthink.
3. **Write where you're blocked** under each category.
4. Identify your **primary bottleneck** (the one causing the biggest slowdown).
5. Write your **first correction step**: the smallest, cleanest action that removes resistance.
6. Use AI to help you build:
   - a visibility plan for Awareness
   - a systems plan for Capacity
   - a mindset upgrade for Identity
   - an offer refinement for Delivery
7. Bring this worksheet into **every monthly CEO review**. Your bottleneck shifts as you grow.

This is the worksheet that prevents burnout, misdiagnosis, and "working harder for no results." This is where your real acceleration begins.

A — Awareness Bottleneck (Visibility)

Do people even know you exist?

Symptoms:
☐ low views
☐ inconsistently posting
☐ unclear message
☐ small audience

Where I'm blocked: _____

C — Capacity Bottleneck (Time/Energy)

You're overwhelmed, overworking, or under-supported.

Symptoms:
- ☐ burnout
- ☐ too many offers
- ☐ no systems
- ☐ can't keep up

Where I'm blocked: _____

I — Identity Bottleneck (Beliefs)

Internal limitations or underpricing.

Symptoms:
- ☐ fear of raising prices
- ☐ impostor syndrome
- ☐ perfectionism
- ☐ staying "small"

Where I'm blocked: _____

D — Delivery Bottleneck (Offer/Systems)

The offer isn't refined or doesn't scale.

Symptoms:
- ☐ not getting results
- ☐ unclear transformation
- ☐ poor onboarding
- ☐ too time-consuming

Where I'm blocked: _____

My Primary Bottleneck Is:

My First Correction Step:

WORKSHEET 7
THE TIMELINE COLLAPSE PLANNER
"12-Month · 6-Month · 90-Day Acceleration Maps"

This worksheet is where you stop building your business on linear time… and start building it on **quantum time**. Most people spread their goals across five years because it feels "safer." Millionaires collapse those timelines by upgrading:

- their identity
- their systems
- their standards
- their offers
- their daily execution

This worksheet turns your 5-year plan into three acceleration windows:

12-Month Collapse Path - (Your "I rewrite the entire trajectory of my life this year" plan.)
6-Month Collapse Path - (Your "I move faster than the industry average" plan.)
90-Day Power Path - (Your "everything changes in a quarter" plan.)

HOW TO USE THIS WORKSHEET
Before filling it out, run the prompts from:

- **The 5-Year Path to $1M**
- **Scaling Pathways (3 Models)**
- **Bottlenecks & Breakpoints**
- **Audience Size vs. Income**

These give you the data you need to collapse the timeline. **Then fill out each section clearly and boldly:**

1. 12-Month Collapse Path

Ask AI: **"What needs to be true for me to hit my 5-year goals in 12 months?"**

Then write:

- the 3 biggest structural changes
- the 1 identity shift that unlocks acceleration
- the non-negotiables you must embody

This is your "impossible becomes inevitable" plan.

2. 6-Month Collapse Path

Ask AI: **"What would a 6-month acceleration demand from me?"**

Then identify:

- the 3 core actions
- what must be eliminated immediately
- where speed requires precision, not chaos

This is the phase where you choose intensity without burnout.

3. 90-Day Power Path

Ask AI: **"What can I accomplish in 90 days that would change everything?"**

Then define:
- the 3 moves that create maximum leverage
- the identity you must embody for the next 90 days
- the standard you operate from

Your 90-day identity is the version of you who doesn't just "try," she **executes like a CEO**.

Final Step

Review this worksheet every quarter. This is the tool that keeps your empire in acceleration mode instead of maintenance mode.

12-Month Collapse Path

"What needs to be true for me to hit my 5-year goals in 12 months?"

I must:

1. _____
2. _____
3. _____

My biggest shift: _____

6-Month Collapse Path

"What would a 6-month acceleration demand from me?"

I must:

1. _____
2. _____
3. _____

What I must stop doing: _____

90-Day Power Path

"What can I accomplish in 90 days that would change everything?"

Top 3 moves:

1. _____
2. _____
3. _____

My 90-day identity: _____

Use this worksheet when:
- you're ready to quantum-leap income
- you want to collapse audience requirements
- you want to build momentum FAST
- you're stepping into a higher identity
- you're eliminating the old version of you
- you're choosing speed, precision, and alignment

This page becomes your most sacred map because it names the version of you who **does not wait five years to become wealthy**.

NOTES:

_____
_____
_____
_____
_____
_____
_____
_____
_____
_____
_____
_____
_____
_____
_____
_____
_____
_____
_____
_____
_____
_____
_____
_____
_____
_____
_____
_____
_____
_____
_____

WORKSHEET 8
THE 5-YEAR MILLIONAIRE VISION TRACKER
"Your Empire Expansion Timeline"

This worksheet is your **panoramic view of wealth**. Not month to month, not quarter to quarter, but **who you become over five years** and the empire you build along the way. Most creators only plan next month. Millionaire women plan **five years ahead with absolute clarity**, but execute as if everything depends on the next 90 days.

This tracker shows you:
- how your income evolves
- how your offers mature
- how your brand deepens
- how your identity expands
- how your role shifts from creator → CEO → empire-builder

This is the moment you stop thinking like a freelancer… and start thinking like a legacy. This is where Step 6 turns from "income planning" into **identity engineering**.

HOW TO USE THIS WORKSHEET

Step 1 — Run your long-range prompts first
Before filling this out, run:
- **The 5-Year Path to $1M+**
- **Revenue Ceilings & Income Potential**
- **Scaling Pathways (3 Models)**
- **Timeline Collapse Prompts**

These give you the clearest picture of what each year actually requires.

Step 2 — Fill out each year with precision
Each year should define three things:
1. **Income Target** — your financial milestone
2. **Focus** — the single strategic priority that moves everything forward
3. **Key Offers** — the products or services that carry your revenue

Keep it simple. Millionaires don't try to do everything at once, they build in seasons.

Step 3 — Write your 5-Year Identity Statement
This is the most important part. Your business cannot outgrow your identity. This statement should capture:
- who you are becoming
- how you think
- how you lead
- what you expect from yourself
- the standards you refuse to lower
- the wealth frequency you operate from

Write it in the tone of a woman who already became her future self and is simply remembering.

Step 4 — Revisit this tracker every 6 months

As you grow, this evolves. Your vision expands. Your numbers change. Your identity upgrades. This worksheet becomes the highest-level roadmap for your entire empire.

YEAR 1 — Foundation

Income Target: _____

Focus: _____

Key Offers: _____

YEAR 2 — Stability

Income Target: _____

Focus: _____

Key Offers: _____

YEAR 3 — Scaling

Income Target: _____

Focus: _____

Key Offers: _____

YEAR 4 — Expansion

Income Target: _____

Focus: _____

Key Offers: _____

YEAR 5 — Empire

Income Target: _____

Focus: _____

Key Offers: _____

5-Year Identity Statement

("Who do I become in the process?")

_____

_____

_____

_____

CLOSING NOTE

This is the moment where wealth becomes structural.

Not emotional.
Not chaotic.
Not "hope-driven."

Structured.
Measured.
Predicted.
Aligned.
Intentional.
Inevitable.

You are no longer guessing.
You are building.
You are pacing.
You are scaling with intelligence, strategy, and clarity.

Your millionaire timeline begins here and Step 7 turns you into the woman who executes it.

STEP 7:

The Daily CEO Prompts

"Prompts to Ask AI Every Day to Stay Focused, Productive, and Consistent"

You've built the foundation.
You've built the vision.
You've built the strategy.

Now it's time to build the *momentum*.

Step 7 is where your identity becomes consistent action.
Where your clarity becomes direction.
Where your strategy becomes daily execution.

Most women lose momentum because they:

- Overthink
- Avoid
- Spiral
- Get distracted
- Focus on the wrong tasks
- Try to do everything
- Work without direction
- Or wake up and "wing it"

This step eliminates that entirely.

Here, AI becomes your:

- daily prioritizer
- bottleneck remover
- revenue strategist
- focus filter
- identity anchor
- execution partner

This is the step that turns your empire into something you build every single day.

Welcome to your Daily CEO Operating System.

TEACHING PAGE:
THE TRUTH ABOUT DAILY MOMENTUM

Success is not built in big leaps. It's built in aligned days. The women who scale aren't the ones who hustle harder. They're the ones who stay in motion, consistently, without burning out. Momentum is created by:

- clarity
- simplicity
- direction
- intentional work
- identity-led choices
- micro-actions done daily

Momentum is lost through:

- reactivity
- overwhelm
- confusion
- perfectionism
- shiny object syndrome
- working on everything except what matters
- chaotic, unstructured action

Daily momentum depends on one truth: **The way you start your day determines the way you lead your business.**

And the way you end your day determines how quickly you grow. Step 7 teaches you to use AI to structure your mornings, direct your days, and recalibrate your evenings, so momentum becomes your default state.

YOUR CEO OPERATING SYSTEM

Your business does not grow because you work harder. It grows because you operate differently.
Your CEO operating system is:

- how you make decisions
- how you choose priorities
- what you focus on
- how quickly you remove bottlenecks
- how consistently you show up
- how intentionally you move toward money
- how grounded you are in your identity

Most women run their business from "task mode."
CEOs run their business from "operating system mode."
Your operating system includes:

1. Morning Clarity
Your priorities, power, and identity for the day.

2. Daily Direction
Your revenue move + your aligned actions.

3. Bottleneck Removal
Instead of pushing through resistance, you dissolve it.

4. Delegation to AI
You stop doing what AI can do faster, better, cleaner.

5. Identity Alignment
You act as the woman who already lives your millionaire life.

6. Evening Integration
You end your day with clarity and confidence not chaos.

When all six pieces align, your business becomes:
- predictable
- scalable
- profitable
- calm
- and actually enjoyable

This step gives you the prompts and structure to run your life and business like a CEO, not a performer, not a perfectionist, not a chaotic achiever.

IDENTITY ACTIVATION

Become the Woman Who Leads.

Every morning, before the tasks, before the noise, before the world tells you who to be: You remind yourself who you already are. You are stepping into the identity of a woman who:

- decides with clarity
- creates with intention
- executes with confidence
- leads with calm focus
- moves with purpose
- builds with consistency

You are not just "running a business."

You are running an empire. And empires are built one aligned day at a time.

HOW TO USE THIS WORKBOOK

Every day, before you react to anything: messages, notifications, tasks, clients, ideas, open AI and ask:

"Act as my Daily CEO Advisor. Base your answers on Steps 1–6 of The AI Empire Builder. Give me clear, simple, aligned guidance."

Then ask 5–10 prompts from this step.

Move slowly.
Notice what feels aligned.
Follow the clarity.

Every evening, ask the reflection prompts.
This resets your nervous system and compounds your momentum.

This step is not about discipline.
It's about consistency without force.
It's about becoming a woman who leads herself powerfully every single day.

MORNING RITUAL PROMPTS
(Your momentum activator)

Your morning shapes your entire day. Your focus, your energy, your priorities, your leadership, they're all set in the first moments you choose to be intentional instead of reactive.

The Morning Ritual Prompts are designed to anchor you into clarity before the world has a chance to pull you off course. This is your moment to lead. To choose. To direct your energy with purpose instead of noise.

These prompts help you begin the day with:
- a clear priority
- aligned action
- grounded identity
- strategic direction
- emotional simplicity
- CEO-level focus

Before you open your inbox. Before you react to messages. Before you let your day be shaped by anything external.

This page exists to help you start every day as the woman who is building her empire, not the woman who is trying to catch up to her life.

INSTRUCTIONS

Every morning, open AI and use these prompts to set your focus, your direction, and your identity for the day.

Steps:
1. Sit for one minute of stillness. Breathe.
2. Copy 2–4 prompts into AI.
3. Add:
   "Answer as my Daily CEO Advisor. Keep it simple, aligned, and strategic."
4. Read the answers slowly.
5. Pick your ONE true priority.
6. Choose your ONE revenue-driving action.
7. Identify anything you can delegate to AI immediately.
8. Move into your day with clarity and purpose.

This ritual should take **3–5 minutes** and will save you hours of wasted energy and scattered effort.

Use it daily. Consistency creates momentum.

MINDSET/MOTIVATION

Every woman who builds an empire has a moment in her morning where she chooses who she is going to be today.

Not the version of her who gets overwhelmed.
Not the version who reacts.
Not the version who spirals or waits or hopes today "goes well."

But the version who leads.

The morning is where you claim your identity:

- "I start my day grounded, focused, and in my power."
- "I choose direction instead of chaos."
- "I choose clarity over confusion."
- "I choose aligned action instead of busywork."
- "I choose the woman I am becoming instead of the woman I used to be."

Your morning ritual is not about productivity.
It's about remembering your power before the world distracts you from it.

Start here.
Lead from here.
And everything else aligns.

These prompts set your direction, focus, energy, and priorities before the world can sway you.

Ask AI:

1. "What is my #1 priority today?"
2. "What's the highest-impact action I can take?"
3. "What can I stop doing so today feels lighter?"
4. "What is my revenue-driving action today?"
5. "Where am I overcomplicating things?"
6. "What would the million-dollar version of me focus on first?"
7. "What can I delegate to AI immediately?"
8. "What boundary will keep me in my power today?"
9. "What's the simplest way to make progress right now?"

Use these to choose your direction.
Do not start your day without them.

EVENING RITUAL PROMPTS

(Your integration anchor)

Your evening determines your momentum far more than your morning.

Most women end their day in:

- Overthinking
- self-criticism
- unfinished tasks
- anxiety loops
- mental clutter

And then they wonder why the next morning feels heavy. Ending your day intentionally is how you create emotional safety, clarity, confidence, and direction. This is where you integrate the day, reset your system, and prepare your mind for a powerful tomorrow.

The Evening Ritual Prompts help you:

- acknowledge progress
- detach from pressure
- collect insights
- regulate your energy
- identify patterns
- reset your focus
- close the day with truth instead of chaos

This ritual becomes your grounding anchor. The thing that keeps you from spiraling, quitting, or collapsing under the weight of your own expectations. This is where growth stops feeling forceful and starts feeling natural.

INSTRUCTIONS

Use these prompts at the end of your workday or before bed to close your mental loops and anchor into clarity.

Steps:

1. Take one slow breath. Let the day soften.
2. Ask 2–4 of the prompts in AI.
3. Add: **"Answer objectively, without shame or judgment. Keep the tone supportive and clear."**
4. Read the answers gently like feedback, not criticism.
5. Identify your wins.
6. Identify your patterns.
7. Choose *one* thing to release.

8. Choose *one* thing to prioritize tomorrow.
9. Close your day with confidence instead of chaos.

This ritual takes **3 minutes** and transforms the way you wake up the next morning.

It keeps you grounded, focused, and moving forward without burnout.

MINDSET/MOTIVATION

A powerful day doesn't end when the work ends, it ends when *you* decide to close it.

The evening ritual is where you reclaim your narrative:
- "I did enough."
- "I learned something valuable today."
- "I am allowed to rest."
- "I trust myself to continue tomorrow."
- "I honor the work I did, not the work I didn't do."

This is not a place for shame or pressure. This is a place for truth.

Every woman building an empire needs a moment at the end of her day where she:
- lets go
- integrates
- re-centers
- releases what's not hers to carry
- and acknowledges the power of even small steps

You become unstoppable not by doing more but by ending your day with clarity, confidence, and self-respect. Your evening ritual is the moment you choose peace over pressure. And that choice compounds your momentum. These prompts help you close the day rooted in clarity, confidence, and truth. Not shame, chaos, or confusion.

Ask AI:
1. "What went well today?"
2. "What slowed me down — and how can I avoid repeating it?"
3. "What am I proud of?"
4. "What clarity did I gain today?"
5. "What felt aligned?"
6. "What needs my attention tomorrow?"
7. "What should I release so tomorrow feels lighter?"
8. "What's one win I'm underestimating?"

This is how you grow without force. This is how you end each day with a clear mind instead of spiraling.

DAILY CEO PROMPTS
(Your operating system in action)

Your Daily CEO Prompts act as the operating system behind your decisions, your focus, your energy, and your execution. They are the questions that bring you back to truth any time you get overwhelmed, distracted, stuck, or uncertain. These prompts are designed to help you:
- clarify your priorities
- identify your revenue-generating actions
- remove the bottlenecks slowing you down
- delegate tasks to AI instead of burning out
- stay aligned with the woman you're becoming
- move through your day with strategic intention
- end each day with growth, not self-pressure

The Daily CEO Prompts are your recalibration tool. You can use them in the morning to set direction, midday to reset your focus, or evening to integrate and reflect. This is not busywork. This is leadership.

These prompts help you anchor into power instead of pressure…
into clarity instead of chaos…
into identity instead of insecurity…
and into aligned execution instead of reactive effort.

Use them whenever your mind feels noisy, your energy feels scattered, or your motivation dips.
They will pull you back into momentum every single time.

INSTRUCTIONS
You can use the Daily CEO Prompts as often as you need:
- in the morning
- between tasks
- when you feel overwhelmed
- when you're unsure what to do next
- when your energy drops
- when your focus slips
- at the end of the day

Steps:
1. Open AI.
2. Choose the category you need: **Clarity, Revenue, Bottlenecks, Delegation, Identity, or Reflection.**
3. Copy 1–3 prompts into AI.
4. Add this instruction: **"Answer as my Daily CEO Advisor. Keep your guidance simple, strategic, and aligned with my goals."**
5. Read the responses slowly.
6. Identify the ONE action that matters most.
7. Do that first.
8. Repeat as needed throughout your day.

These prompts are designed to shift your state in under 60 seconds. Use them anytime your mind feels cluttered or your direction feels unclear. This is your in-the-moment power tool.

MINDSET / MOTIVATION

Every time you ask these prompts, you are choosing to lead yourself like a woman who builds an empire. You're choosing clarity over confusion. Direction over chaos. Identity over impulse. Power over panic. Strategy over spiraling.

These prompts are not just questions, they're mirrors. They show you:
- where you're aligned
- where you're drifting
- where you're hiding
- where you're underestimating yourself
- where money wants to come in
- where you need to step up as the wealthier version of you

This is the moment in your day where you pause and say:
- "I don't run my business from anxiety. I run it from clarity."
- "I don't make decisions from fear. I make them from identity."
- "I don't chase everything. I choose what matters."
- "I am the woman who leads with intention."

Your empire is not built in dramatic bursts of effort, it's built in these small, consistent moments where you choose to be her. Every time you use these prompts, you strengthen the identity of the CEO you are becoming. And THAT is what creates momentum. That is what creates results. That is what makes your success inevitable.

CLARITY PROMPTS
1. "What is my true priority today?"
2. "What feels urgent but doesn't actually matter?"
3. "What is the one thing that would make everything else easier?"
4. "Where am I wasting energy?"
5. "What can I simplify?"
6. "How do I simplify today?"
7. "What is the single highest-impact action I can take today?"
8. "What am I avoiding that would move the needle the most?"
9. "What would the million-dollar version of me focus on first?"
10. "What's one thing I can finish today that will make me proud tonight?"
11. "What can I release so today feels lighter and more effective?"

REVENUE PROMPTS
1. "What offer wants attention right now?"
2. "Where is the easiest money I'm ignoring?"
3. "What is my simplest revenue-generating action today?"
4. "What content would increase demand today?"
5. "What's one fast win that moves money closer?"

6. "What could I improve today that would increase sales?"
7. "What client, product, or offer needs nurturing today?"
8. "What small step today supports long-term revenue?"

BOTTLENECK PROMPTS
1. "What's blocking me today?"
2. "What resistance am I feeling and why?"
3. "What am I avoiding that would get me unstuck?"
4. "What outdated belief is influencing me?"
5. "What would make this 10x easier?"
6. "What's my bottleneck today and what's the easiest way to solve it?"
7. "What am I overcomplicating right now?"
8. "What task is draining me that I could simplify or eliminate?"
9. "What resistance am I feeling and why?"
10. "What expectation can I release to create space and ease?"
11. "What system, habit, or pattern needs upgrading today?"

DELEGATION PROMPTS
1. "What should AI handle for me right now?"
2. "What am I doing manually that AI can automate?"
3. "What tasks are draining my time and energy?"
4. "What content, systems, or assets can AI build for me today?"
5. "What tasks are beneath my CEO identity and should be delegated?"
6. "What systems can AI set up or improve right now?"
7. "What decisions can AI help me make more efficiently?"

IDENTITY PROMPTS
1. "What energy am I meant to embody right now?"
2. "What action aligns with my future identity?"
3. "What decision would I be proud of in 24 hours?"
4. "How does the wealthy, successful version of me move today?"
5. "What boundary do I need to hold today?"
6. "What am I choosing today because it feels aligned, not pressured?"
7. "What would make today feel powerful and grounded?"
8. "What truth do I need to remember about myself today?"

REFLECTION & INTEGRATION PROMPTS
1. "What went well yesterday and how can I build on it?"
2. "What slowed me down yesterday and how can I avoid repeating it?"
3. "What am I proud of myself for?"
4. "What clarity did I gain yesterday that informs today?"
5. "What did I learn about my energy, habits, or patterns?"
6. "What do I want to do differently today?"
7. "What progress am I underestimating?"

WHAT TO ASK AI WHEN YOU'RE STUCK

(*The Overwhelm Rescue Page*)

Every entrepreneur hits moments when their brain stalls. When everything feels heavy, confusing, pointless, or impossible. When decisions feel too big, tasks feel like mountains, and clarity disappears. Overwhelm isn't a sign that something is wrong. It's a sign that your nervous system is overloaded. This page is your reset button. These prompts are designed to pull you out of:

- Spiraling
- Perfectionism
- Paralysis
- Shame
- Frustration
- Exhaustion
- emotional over-identification
- "I don't know what to do next" loops

They help you:

- strip the noise
- zoom out
- find the truth
- soften the pressure
- reconnect with your power
- choose your simplest next aligned step

These questions interrupt the mental chaos and recalibrate you back into clarity, compassion, and forward movement. This is the page that keeps women from quitting. The page that brings you back to yourself. The page that resets your mind faster than anything else. Keep this section close. Use it anytime your brain feels too loud to move.

INSTRUCTIONS

Use these prompts the moment you feel:

- overwhelmed
- frozen
- unmotivated
- confused
- tired
- emotionally flooded
- stuck in perfectionism
- unsure what to do next

Steps:

1. Pause for a moment.
2. Open AI.
3. Copy 1–3 of the prompts into the chat.
4. Add this instruction: **"Answer gently, clearly, and objectively. Help me see the truth without judgment."**
5. Read the response slowly not as criticism, but as clarity.

6. Choose the *simplest* next step.
7. Take one small action or allow yourself the rest you need.
8. Let the pressure melt. Let the clarity return.

These prompts work best when you surrender the expectation to "perform" and allow yourself to receive support. They're designed to regulate your nervous system, not push you harder.

MINDSET / MOTIVATION

Being stuck doesn't mean you're failing. It means your body and mind are signaling for a shift. You are not behind. You are not broken. You are not "bad at this." You're simply overwhelmed and overwhelm is a temporary state, not an identity. These prompts remind you:

- "I don't need to have the whole plan right now."
- "I only need my next aligned step."
- "I'm allowed to choose ease."
- "I'm allowed to release pressure."
- "I'm allowed to rest without losing momentum."
- "I can recalibrate at any moment."
- "I can ask for clarity instead of forcing it."

When you're stuck, your job isn't to push harder, your job is to reconnect with yourself. The truth is: You don't get unstuck through force. You get unstuck through gentleness, awareness, and a single simple step in the right direction.

Let these prompts guide you back to clarity. Let them remind you of your power. Let them soften the noise long enough for you to hear your own wisdom again. Your empire doesn't crumble when you pause. It strengthens when you return aligned.

These are your emergency prompts. The ones you use when you're spiraling, frozen, frustrated, tired, or completely unmotivated.

Ask AI:
1. "What is the REAL problem here?"
2. "What's the simplest possible next step?"
3. "What am I trying to do perfectly instead of simply?"
4. "What expectation can I release right now?"
5. "What am I making this mean that isn't true?"
6. "What do I need: clarity, rest, or direction?"
7. "What is the kindest choice I can make for myself?"
8. "What would future-me tell me to do next?"
9. "If I made this easy, how would I approach it?"
10. "What do I actually want right now?"

This page alone saves women from quitting. It resets your nervous system instantly.

WEEKLY CEO CALIBRATION
(Your 7-day reset + alignment check)

Weekly calibration is how you grow with intention instead of chaos. Most women build their businesses day by day without ever stopping to look at the bigger picture. They operate from urgency instead of clarity, reaction instead of strategy, and emotion instead of truth. Weekly CEO Calibration is your reset. Your check-in. Your clarity anchor.

This process helps you:
- assess what's working
- identify what's not
- recognize your patterns
- track your emotional + energetic trends
- catch yourself drifting
- reconnect to your identity
- refine your direction
- choose aligned priorities for the next week

This is how you ensure your growth is not accidental, it's intentional.

When you calibrate weekly, you:
- compound your progress
- move faster with less effort
- stop repeating the same blocks
- stay deeply aligned with your goals
- move forward without spiraling
- build confidence through awareness
- make better decisions with clarity

This is the difference between women who "try" to build a business and women who actually scale one. Your week isn't complete until you calibrate.

INSTRUCTIONS

Once a week, ideally the same day every week, take 10 quiet minutes to ask AI: **"Give me my Weekly CEO Review based on my progress, energy, clarity, habits, and goals."**

Then move through each prompt slowly and honestly.

Steps:
1. Sit somewhere calm.
2. Ask the Weekly Review prompt.
3. Copy the 10 calibration questions into AI.
4. Add this note: **"Answer objectively and kindly. Focus on clarity, not judgment."**
5. Read AI's reflections carefully.
6. Identify your patterns.

7. Choose ONE thing to stop and ONE thing to start.
8. Clarify your revenue focus for the next week.
9. Ask AI for any tools, assets, content, or systems you need.
10. End by visualizing your next-week identity.

This is your strategic reset. Your moment to step out of the noise and into leadership.

MINDSET / MOTIVATION

A woman who calibrates weekly never stays lost for long. This ritual isn't about perfection. It's about awareness. You are not judging yourself. You are witnessing yourself with honesty, compassion, and clarity. Weekly calibration is the moment where you step into the identity of the woman who:

- notices her patterns
- acknowledges her wins
- course-corrects gently
- chooses her priorities intentionally
- leads herself with emotional maturity
- makes decisions like the wealthiest version of her
- and refuses to coast unconsciously through her life

This process is not about fixing yourself, it's about understanding yourself. It's about recognizing:

- "I don't need to be perfect to move forward."
- "I just need to be aware."
- "I can refine instead of restart."
- "I can adjust instead of collapse."
- "I can build momentum without force."

This is how you build a life you're proud of. This is how you build a business you can sustain. This is how you step into the identity of the woman who leads with confidence and clarity. Weekly calibration makes your growth inevitable.

Once a week, ask AI: **"Give me my Weekly CEO Review based on my progress, energy, clarity, and goals."**

Then go through these:
1. What were my biggest wins this week?
2. What patterns slowed me down?
3. What decisions strengthened my identity?
4. Where did I drift out of alignment?
5. What bottleneck keeps appearing?
6. What's one thing I must stop doing next week?
7. What's one thing I must start doing?
8. What's my revenue focus for next week?
9. What support do I need from AI?
10. What would make next week feel powerful?

This keeps your trajectory clean, intentional, and upward.

WORKSHEET:
MY DAILY CEO DASHBOARD

This worksheet helps you anchor your day in clarity, focus, and aligned action. Use it each morning to choose your priorities and each evening to integrate your wins and insights.

How to use:
Fill this out once in the morning and once again at night. Keep your answers simple, specific, and aligned with the identity you're stepping into.

Today's Top Priority:

_____

My 3 High-Impact Actions:

    1. _____

    2. _____

    3. _____

Today's Revenue Driver:

_____

Today's Bottleneck:

_____

What I'm Delegating to AI:

_____

Identity I'm Leading From Today:

_____

How I Will Keep Myself Out of Chaos:

_____

Tonight's Reflection:

_____

_____

WORKSHEET:
WEEKLY CEO SNAPSHOT

This weekly snapshot helps you zoom out, evaluate your progress, and recalibrate your direction. It gives you a clear, honest view of your patterns, your wins, and your next aligned steps.

How to use:
Complete this once a week after your Weekly CEO Calibration. Answer honestly, without judgment. Awareness is what drives the next level.

My Wins:

My Sticking Points:

What I'm Releasing:

Next Week's Focus:

Next Week's Revenue Move:

Who I Am Becoming:

CLOSING NOTE

You are no longer building your business through force.
You are building it through clarity, consistency, and identity-led action.

You are no longer guessing.
You are choosing.

You are stepping into your power daily,
and this daily operating system keeps you aligned with the woman you are becoming.

Your empire grows because you grow.
Your momentum compounds because your clarity is consistent.
Your success is inevitable because you lead yourself like a CEO.

This is where consistency becomes your superpower.
And Step 8 builds from here.

STEP 8:

The Automation & AI Team Builder

"Prompts to Build Automations, Workflows, Systems & SOPs Using AI"

Welcome to the step that separates hustlers from CEOs.

You've done the mindset work.
You've found your purpose.
You've generated your ideas.
You've mapped your empire.
You've anchored your daily CEO identity.

Now it's time to scale like a woman who refuses to do everything alone.

Step 8 is where AI becomes your **team**,
your **systems department**,
your **workflow engineer**,
your **operations brain**,
your **content machine**,
your **marketing strategist**,
your **automation engine**,
and your *full in-house support staff.*

This is where your business stops relying on willpower
and starts relying on infrastructure.

This is where your empire gets lighter
because your systems get stronger.

This is where you step fully into the identity of a woman who leads
not by force,
not by burnout,
but by *design*.

WHAT STEP 8 IS

This is the step where everything changes. Up until now, you've been evolving your identity, your ideas, your clarity, your direction, and your daily CEO habits. But Step 8 is where you stop building your business with *your hands* and start building it with *your systems*. This is where AI becomes your **team.**

Your:
- Strategist
- Marketer
- Copywriter
- Designer
- Operations manager
- Systems architect
- Automation engine

No more doing everything manually. No more relying on energy, mood, or motivation. No more building from chaos or pressure. Step 8 gives you the prompts to build **workflows, SOPs, automations, templates, funnels, and systems** that run even when you're resting, busy, tired, emotional, or uninspired. This is the step that frees you. This is where your business becomes lighter, more profitable, more consistent, because your systems do the work with you, and for you.

This is the moment you shift from "I'm building a business"
to
"I'm building an empire that runs without exhausting me."

Step 8 teaches you to use AI to:
- build workflows
- create SOPs
- automate repetitive tasks
- design marketing systems
- build funnels
- structure content calendars
- automate lead generation
- create tracking dashboards
- build templates
- turn chaos into clarity
- turn effort into process
- turn pressure into ease

This is the step that frees your time, your mind, your energy, and your nervous system. This is where AI stops being a tool and becomes your team.

IDENTITY ACTIVATION

Become the Woman Who Doesn't Do It All, She Delegates All

This step isn't about grinding harder. It's about installing systems that work for you, whether you're active, resting, busy, emotional, inspired, or offline.

You are stepping into the identity of a woman who:
- works less but accomplishes more
- refuses tasks beneath her CEO identity
- delegates easily
- builds scalable systems
- uses AI as leverage
- values her time like a millionaire
- chooses simplicity
- creates workflows that run without her

You are not here to be the worker. You're here to be the architect.

HOW TO USE THIS WORKBOOK

Each page in Step 8 gives you a set of prompts to ask AI when you want to build:
- a workflow
- an SOP
- a system
- a funnel
- a content engine
- an automation
- a dashboard
- a template
- a process
- a structure that saves you 20 hours a week

To use each section:

1. Copy the prompt into AI.
2. Add the instruction:
   "Answer as if you are my full operations team building scalable systems based on my personality, workflow preferences, energy, lifestyle, and revenue goals."
3. Review the result.
4. Keep only what feels aligned, simple, sustainable, and empowering.
5. Tell AI to refine, shorten, expand, or simplify until it fits your flow.

This is your systems lab.
Your operations studio.
Your automation command center.

THE TRUTH ABOUT AUTOMATION

Women don't burn out because they're incapable. They burn out because they're doing **12 jobs alone** that AI can do instantly.

Automation isn't cold.
Automation is support.
Automation is protection.
Automation is feminine leadership.
Automation is ease.
Automation is power.

AI was built to carry the workload, so *you* can carry the vision.

This page is where you shift out of:
- constant effort
- manual labor
- doing everything yourself
- feeling behind
- relying on motivation
- inconsistent output

And into:
- systems that hold you
- workflows that repeat automatically
- content engines that never run dry
- templates that save hours
- SOPs that prevent chaos
- automation that works even when you don't

Your business cannot scale on effort. It scales on structure.
Your empire cannot be built on pressure. It builds itself on systems.
Your income cannot grow through manual hustle. It grows through automation that multiplies your output.

This step teaches you **how to think like a CEO who never does unnecessary work.**

You are not here to be the worker. You are here to be the architect.
You're not here to do all the tasks. You're here to build the systems that do them.

This is where your business stops relying on your energy and starts relying on its infrastructure.
This is where your empire becomes inevitable.

THE AI TEAM BUILDER PROMPTS

If you've never used AI like this before, here's exactly how these prompts work.

Most people use AI like a search engine. Step 8 teaches you to use AI like a **full internal team.** These prompts show AI *how to think*, *how to behave*, and *how to work* in each role you assign it. When you select a role (Content Marketer, SEO Expert, Copywriter, etc.), you are essentially telling AI:

"Step into this job and complete it for me."

AI then uses:
- your voice
- your goals
- your business model
- your audience
- your brand identity
- your workflow
- your personality

…to produce work as if you hired an actual expert.

Here's how these prompts function, even for a total beginner:

1. You choose the department you need help with.

Marketing? Sales? Workflow? Launch planning? There's a category for each.

2. You copy one of the prompts into AI.

That prompt tells AI the *role* it must play.

3. AI generates the work instantly.

It will give you:
- calendars
- funnels
- workflows
- templates
- content
- email sequences
- launch plans
- systems
- SOPs
- automations

…without you needing to know how to create any of these yourself.

You don't need experience. You don't need to know the "right" words. You don't need technical skills. The prompts *do the thinking for you.*

4. You refine by giving AI simple direction.

You can say:
- "shorter"
- "more playful"
- "simpler"
- "more confident"
- "make this fit my energy"
- "rewrite using my brand voice"

AI will adjust everything instantly.

5. The role-based sections keep you organized.

Instead of guessing what to ask, you pick the department that matches what you need.

If you want content → go to "Content Marketer"
If you want clarity → go to "Operations Manager"
If you want sales → go to "Sales Strategist"
If you want automation → go to "Automation Engineer"

Each section is like walking into a different office in your digital headquarters.

6. You can use these prompts daily or whenever needed.

Feeling stuck in content? Tell AI to be your marketer.
Overwhelmed by emails? Tell AI to be your copywriter.
Need a workflow? Tell AI to be your operations manager.
You don't need to build a team. You already have one. Right here.

7. The more you use these prompts, the smarter your AI becomes.

AI learns:
- your voice
- your preferences
- your style
- your patterns
- your energy
- your brand

Within days, it starts writing, planning, and structuring things *exactly the way you like them.*

BOTTOM LINE

These prompts are not random. They are **job assignments.** You are giving AI a role, a task, and a purpose.

AI becomes the team so you can become the CEO.

These prompts work for **any skill level**, any industry, any business model, any stage of growth.

They remove overwhelm, decision fatigue, and busywork, so you can lead from clarity and power.

SECTION 1
AI as Your Content Marketer

Turn AI into the strategist that builds your content systems for you.

Most women waste hours trying to create content from scratch: brainstorming ideas, rewriting posts, guessing what their audience wants, or posting inconsistently because it feels overwhelming. This section eliminates all of that.

Here, AI takes over as your **full content marketing department**, handling:
- planning
- strategy
- idea generation
- repurposing
- visibility routines
- brand voice analysis
- calendar creation

Instead of trying to figure out what to post, how often, and why, AI does the heavy lifting for you. You're not just getting ideas. You're getting a *system*.

A system that:

✓ keeps your content consistent

✓ increases demand for your offers

✓ matches your energy and lifestyle

✓ works even when you don't feel inspired

✓ saves hours of mental load every week

This is where AI becomes your strategist not just your writer.

HOW TO USE THESE PROMPTS

Use this section anytime you need to:
- create content faster
- stay consistent
- build a content plan
- repurpose posts
- define your brand voice
- increase visibility
- scale content without burnout

INSTRUCTIONS

1. Choose one prompt from the list.

2. Paste it into AI.

3. Add this line: **"Use my brand voice, my audience, and my goals to create a content system I can sustain."**

4. Read the response and refine by saying:

    o   "Simplify this."

    o   "Make it match my personality."

    o   "Turn this into templates I can reuse."

    o   "Make this fit a 20-minute daily routine."

5. Save the resulting systems in one place. this becomes your ongoing content engine.

PROMPTS TO BUILD YOUR CONTENT SYSTEMS

1. "Create a 30-day content calendar based on my offers, audience, and goals."

2. "Generate 20 pieces of content that drive demand for my main offer."

3. "Build a content system I can maintain in 20 minutes a day."

4. "Repurpose this post into 10 formats: Reel, carousel, email, caption, blog, etc."

5. "Analyze my content voice and create a style guide."

6. "Build a weekly visibility routine based on my energy and lifestyle."

SECTION 2
AI as Your SEO Expert

Let AI handle the visibility, traffic, and discoverability you shouldn't be doing manually.

SEO is one of the most overwhelming parts of business for most women. Complicated terms, endless tutorials, outdated strategies, and the fear of "doing it wrong."

This section removes all of that pressure. Here, AI becomes your **SEO department**, responsible for:
- keyword research
- content optimization
- organic visibility
- long-term traffic planning
- website analysis
- SEO checklists
- improving discoverability

Instead of guessing what Google wants or how to get your content seen, AI will:

✓ find your keywords

✓ organize them by intent

✓ build a 3-month traffic plan

✓ rewrite posts to be SEO-friendly but still human

✓ give you improvements you'd never spot alone

And the best part?

AI makes SEO **simple, clear, repeatable**, and aligned with your voice not robotic or keyword-stuffed. You don't have to become an SEO expert. You just need to ask the right prompts and AI becomes the expert for you.

HOW TO USE THESE PROMPTS

Use this section anytime you want to:
- increase traffic
- improve discoverability
- optimize your blogs or website
- simplify SEO
- build a long-term content strategy
- get seen by the right people

INSTRUCTIONS

1. Choose a prompt from the SEO list.

2. Paste it into AI.

3. Add this line for the best results: **"Keep my tone human, aligned with my brand voice, and not robotic or keyword-stuffed."**

4. If AI gives you something too technical, say:

   o "Simplify this."

   o "Make this actionable for a beginner."

   o "Turn this into steps I can follow."

   o "Put this into a checklist format."

5. Use the SEO plan or checklist as part of your weekly content routine.

AI will handle the complexity. You follow the clarity.

PROMPTS TO AUTOMATE DISCOVERABILITY

1. "Give me SEO keywords for my brand, niche, and offers."

2. "Create a 3-month SEO content plan that drives organic traffic."

3. "Optimize this blog post for SEO without making it robotic."

4. "Build an SEO checklist I can reuse for every piece of content."

5. "Analyze my website and give me SEO improvements."

SECTION 3
AI As Your Brand Designer

Use AI to create a cohesive, recognizable brand that feels like YOU.

Most women struggle with branding because they think they need:

- a graphic design degree
- expensive software
- a perfect aesthetic
- endless template tweaking
- or a professional designer

But branding is not just visuals. Branding is **identity, voice, tone, resonance, emotion, and consistency.**
This section turns AI into your **full brand design department**, giving you:

- a brand identity guide
- your emotional tone + archetype
- voice guidelines
- color story inspiration
- messaging pillars
- content templates
- consistency across platforms

Instead of guessing what "your brand" should look or feel like, AI will analyze YOU…
your personality, your mission, your values, and your audience…
and turn it into a cohesive, elevated, unforgettable brand.

This saves you hours of trial and error and makes your content feel magnetic, polished, and instantly recognizable. AI doesn't just design for you. It translates who you are into a brand that supports your empire.

HOW TO USE THESE PROMPTS

Use this section when you want to:

- define your brand identity
- refine your voice
- create templates
- make your content cohesive
- prepare for a relaunch or rebrand
- clarify your message
- build a recognizable aesthetic

INSTRUCTIONS

1. Pick one of the prompts from the Brand Designer list.
2. Paste it into AI with this instruction: **"Base this on my personality, message, audience, and natural communication style."**
3. Review what AI gives you and refine by saying:
   - "Make this simpler."
   - "Make this more confident/playful/luxury/edgy."

- "Turn this into reusable templates."
- "Adjust this to feel more aligned with my energy."

4. Apply your new brand guide to your content, website, bios, and templates.

AI will hold the structure. you bring the soul.

PROMPTS TO KEEP YOUR BRAND COHESIVE

1. "Create a brand identity guide based on my personality and message."

2. "Define my brand voice, tone, archetype, and emotional resonance."

3. "Create templates for my posts, emails, and content pillars."

4. "Design a brand messaging system I can use across platforms."

SECTION 4
AI as Your Copywriter
Write high-converting content, emails, and sales copy in minutes not hours.

Nothing slows entrepreneurs down like writing.

Staring at a blank page.
Trying to be clever.
Overthinking hooks, headlines, captions, emails, and sales pages.
Feeling like everything sounds cringe, boring, or too "salesy."

This section solves all of that instantly.

When AI steps in as your **copywriter**, it becomes the voice behind your:
- sales pages
- landing pages
- emails
- nurture sequences
- social captions
- hooks + headlines
- content ideas
- brand messaging
- templates you can reuse forever

You don't have to write from scratch ever again.
You don't have to guess what sounds good.
You don't have to "sound like someone else."

AI takes your brand voice, YOUR energy, and turns it into magnetic, clear, emotionally intelligent copy that sells without pressure.

This is where your content becomes easy.
This is where writing becomes fast.
This is where every message becomes clear, aligned, and confident.

HOW TO USE THESE PROMPTS

Use this section when you want to:
- write faster
- sound clearer
- feel more confident
- sell without feeling salesy
- automate email sequences
- optimize posts
- create high-converting messaging
- develop templates

INSTRUCTIONS

1. Copy one of the prompts into AI.

2. Add this line:
   "Write this in my natural voice but elevate it to be clearer, more confident, and more magnetic."

3. If the copy feels too formal or too robotic, say:

   o "Make this more conversational."

   o "Add more personality."

   o "Make this bolder/more feminine/more confident/more grounded."

   o "Simplify the language."

4. Ask AI to turn the final version into:

   o a template

   o a reusable framework

   o multiple formats (caption, email, headline, Reel, blog)

You never have to fight the blank page again.
AI will write it.
You will approve it.

PROMPTS TO WRITE EVERYTHING FASTER

1. "Write a sales page based on my offer, audience, and transformation."

2. "Write 20 hooks, headlines, or call-to-actions for my brand."

3. "Write an email sequence that nurtures leads into buyers."

4. "Rewrite this to sound more confident, magnetic, and aligned."

5. "Create copy templates I can reuse forever."

SECTION 5
AI As Your Operations Manager
Let AI bring order, structure, and efficiency to every part of your business.

Operations are where most entrepreneurs fall apart not because they're incapable, but because nobody ever taught them how to build systems, workflows, or organization structures. This section changes that. Here, AI becomes your **full operations department**, responsible for:

- structuring your business
- organizing your projects
- defining your tasks
- creating SOPs
- building workflows
- establishing weekly rhythms
- planning launches
- building project systems
- helping you run your business like a CEO, not a chaotic one-woman show

Think of this as the moment your business stops living inside your head and becomes a *clean, organized, functioning machine.*

Instead of waking up and asking, **"What do I do today?"** you'll have:

✓ clear workflows

✓ weekly CEO rhythms

✓ documented processes

✓ launch systems

✓ business structure

This is the backbone of your empire. This is what gives your creativity ROOM to breathe. AI becomes the operations brain so you can become the visionary.

HOW TO USE THESE PROMPTS

Use this section when you want to:

- get organized
- stop winging your business
- reduce chaos
- prepare for a launch
- systemize recurring tasks
- define your weekly flow
- build workflows that you can actually follow
- free your mind from decision fatigue

INSTRUCTIONS

1. Pick one prompt from the Operations list.

2. Paste it into AI and add this line:
   "Create this system using simplicity, clarity, and my natural working style."

3. Let AI generate the workflow, SOP, or structure.

4. Refine by saying:

   o "Make this simpler."

   o "Shorten the steps."

   o "Organize this into a list or table."

   o "Turn this into something I can follow daily/weekly."

5. Save each workflow or SOP in a digital folder — this becomes your Operations Manual.

When your operations become simple and clear, everything in your life becomes lighter.

You stop running your business from survival mode.
You start running it from strategy.

PROMPTS TO ORGANIZE YOUR ENTIRE BUSINESS

1. "Create a workflow for my content creation system."

2. "Build SOPs for recurring tasks in my business."

3. "Create a weekly CEO schedule based on my goals and energy."

4. "Build a project management system for my next launch."

5. "Create a business organization structure for my current phase."

SECTION 6
AI AS YOUR AUTOMATION ENGINEER

Turn AI into the engine that removes manual work, busywork, and burnout.

This is the section where your business becomes lighter. Most entrepreneurs stay stuck because they're buried under tasks:

- posting manually
- sending follow-up emails
- onboarding clients
- writing reminders
- scheduling content
- answering questions
- managing leads
- repeating the same workflows
- handling admin by hand

This creates burnout, chaos, and inconsistency. But when AI steps in as your **Automation Engineer**, everything changes.

AI will help you:

- automate content scheduling
- automate emails
- automate follow-ups
- automate onboarding
- automate nurture sequences
- automate customer communications
- automate tracking
- automate lead flow
- automate entire business systems

Instead of relying on your energy, memory, or mood, your business starts relying on automation.
This creates:

✓ more time

✓ more freedom

✓ more consistency

✓ more mental space

✓ more revenue with less effort

Automation doesn't replace your humanity, it protects your energy so you can focus on creation, leadership, and alignment. This is where you stop operating like a freelancer and start operating like a CEO with a fully systemized business.

HOW TO USE THESE PROMPTS

Use this section when you want to:
- do less manual work
- build funnels
- optimize your time
- create automations that run without you
- support your clients and customers automatically
- streamline your business
- reduce chaos
- increase consistency

INSTRUCTIONS

1. Choose one automation prompt from the list.
2. Paste it into AI and add this instruction: **"Explain this automation in simple steps and show me how to implement it without overwhelm."**
3. AI will give you:
   o the automation
   o the tools
   o the steps
   o the workflow
   o the setup instructions
4. Refine by asking:
   o "Make this simpler."
   o "Remove unnecessary steps."
   o "Turn this into a beginner-friendly version."
   o "Tell me the easiest way to automate this based on my skill level."
5. Implement the automation or save it for your VA/future team.

Every automation you build frees up hours of your life.

This is how you scale without spending more time.
This is how you grow without sacrificing your energy.
This is how you build a business that takes care of YOU, too.

PROMPTS TO FREE YOU FROM MANUAL WORK

1. "Create automations for content scheduling, emails, and follow-ups."

2. "Build a simple funnel that runs on autopilot."

3. "Design a lead generation system that requires minimal daily effort."

4. "Create a customer onboarding workflow."

5. "Show me where I'm doing manual work AI can automate."

SECTION 7
AI AS YOUR SALES STRATEGIST

Let AI build the revenue systems, demand engines, and sales structures your business needs to grow.

Sales is the part of business that most women avoid not because they can't sell, but because they've never been taught to do it in a way that feels:

- clear
- ethical
- aligned
- simple
- sustainable
- or true to who they are

This section changes that forever.

Here, AI becomes your **full sales strategy department**, responsible for:

- analyzing your offers
- designing simple sales strategies
- building demand
- creating follow-up systems
- mapping your buyer journey
- planning your revenue
- increasing conversions
- helping you sell without pressure

You no longer have to guess:

"What should I sell next?"
"How do I create demand?"
"What content creates buyers?"
"What's my revenue plan?"
"How do I nurture people?"

AI handles all of it.

This is where you shift from *hoping* for sales
to having **systems that create them.**

Your offers become clearer. Your demand becomes consistent. Your conversions increase. Your revenue stabilizes.

AI brings the strategy. You bring the energy.

HOW TO USE THESE PROMPTS

Use this section when you:
- feel unclear about your offer
- want more sales
- need a better sales process
- want easier revenue
- want to increase conversions
- want to create demand
- want to understand your buyer
- want to simplify your sales strategy

INSTRUCTIONS

1. Copy one prompt from the list and paste it into AI.

2. Add this line: **"Make this sales strategy simple, ethical, aligned with my personality, and easy to implement."**

3. Let AI break down the strategy step-by-step.

4. Refine by saying:

   o "Shorten this."

   o "Make this beginner-friendly."

   o "Turn this into a weekly routine."

   o "Show me the easiest version of this."

   o "Make this fit my brand vibe."

5. Implement the strategy or save it as a reusable template.

The clearer your sales system is,
the easier it is to make money consistently,
without forcing, overworking, or posting all day.

PROMPTS FOR REVENUE SYSTEMS

- "Analyze my offer and create a simple sales strategy."

- "Give me 10 ways to create demand this week."

- "Create a follow-up system that increases conversions."

- "Build a revenue plan for the next 90 days."

- "Map a buyer journey based on my brand."

SECTION 8
AI AS YOUR LAUNCH PLANNER

Run stress-free launches with clear steps, simple structure, and zero overwhelm.

Launching is one of the most intimidating parts of business for most women.

The planning…
The prep…
The content…
The emails…
The timing…
The pressure…

It can feel like too much, which leads to procrastination, chaos, or launches that never happen. This section solves all of that.

When AI steps in as your **Launch Planner**, it handles:
- launch strategy
- timelines
- warm-up sequences
- email writing
- content planning
- launch checklists
- pre-launch visibility
- organization
- stress reduction
- messaging clarity

Instead of forcing yourself to figure out the "right" steps of a launch, AI does it all FOR you and breaks it into simple, manageable actions. You get to focus on showing up with confidence and energy, while AI handles the structure, plan, and execution strategy. This is where launching becomes:

✓ calmer

✓ simpler

✓ clearer

✓ shorter

✓ more aligned

✓ and actually doable

No burnout. No confusion. No pressure. Just a launch plan that makes sense and works.

HOW TO USE THESE PROMPTS

Use this section when you want to:
- plan a launch
- run a stress-free launch
- prepare your audience
- write your email sequence
- structure your content
- create your launch timeline
- build clarity around your offer
- turn a launch idea into a step-by-step plan

INSTRUCTIONS

1. Pick a prompt from the list and paste it into AI.

2. Add this line for best results: **"Break this launch plan into clear, simple, low-pressure steps I can follow without overwhelm."**

3. Let AI build your launch timeline, prep content, and email flow.

4. Refine by saying:

   o "Make this shorter."

   o "Reduce the workload."

   o "Turn this into a 7-day/10-day/14-day plan."

   o "Make this aligned with my energy and personality."

   o "Turn this into a checklist I can follow easily."

5. Save the plan as a template you can use for every future launch.

Launching doesn't have to feel like a sprint. It can feel supported, structured, grounded, and powerful. AI holds the staircase. You just take the steps.

Prompts to run stress-free launches

- "Build a 14-day launch plan based on my offer and audience."

- "Create my pre-launch content strategy."

- "Write my launch emails: warm-up, open cart, close cart."

- "Create a launch checklist so I don't miss anything."

- "Design a simple launch that doesn't overwhelm me."

WORKSHEET:
AI SYSTEMS BUILDER DAILY DELEGATION

Use this page to lighten your workload, strengthen your systems, and train your brain to think like a CEO.

This worksheet helps you practice the most important skill in scaling:

letting go of the tasks you should NOT be doing
and
delegating them to AI without hesitation.

Most entrepreneurs stay overwhelmed because they try to handle everything alone.
This worksheet rewires that pattern.

Here, you identify:
- what you're doing manually
- what is draining your time
- what AI can take over immediately
- what workflows you need
- what templates will save hours
- what automations would lighten your whole week

This page is your daily reminder that you're not supposed to carry the entire business on your back.

You are meant to **lead**, not overwork.
You are meant to **delegate**, not drown in tasks.
You are meant to **design the system**, not be the system.

This worksheet shifts you into true CEO mode. The kind where your business supports YOU.

HOW TO USE THIS WORKSHEET

Use this page at the start of your day, or anytime you feel overwhelmed or overloaded.

1. **List your manual tasks.** Write down anything you're doing that feels repetitive, draining, or beneath your CEO identity.

2. **Choose what AI will take over today.** Pick 1–3 items and commit to delegating them immediately.

3. **Decide what workflow AI should build.** This is where you say: *"I never want to manually do this again."*

4. **Identify the SOP or template you need.** This creates long-term efficiency. One template today saves hours every week.

5. **Choose one automation.** Ask yourself: *"What would free me the most if it ran on autopilot?"*

6. **Finish with the emotional check-in.** The last question anchors you into alignment: *What would make my business feel lighter today?* This is your guiding truth.

7. **Give the entire list to AI.** Use a prompt like: **"Build these workflows, templates, and automations for me. Make everything simple, clear, and easy to implement."**

This worksheet helps you build your business with **systems, not stress.**
With **structure, not struggle.**
With **support, not self-sacrifice.**

Today's Manual Tasks I Should NOT Be Doing:

\
\
\

What I'm Delegating to AI Today:

\
\
\

Workflow I Need AI to Build:

\

Template or SOP I Want AI to Create for Me:

\

What Automation Would Save Me the Most Energy Right Now?

\

What Would Make My Business Feel Lighter Today?

\

WORKSHEET:
AI TEAM ROLES & TASKS

Assign tasks to your AI team so YOU stay in your CEO identity.

This worksheet helps you step fully into the identity of a woman who leads with clarity not a woman who tries to do everything herself. The truth is: Most overwhelm comes from not knowing *what* to delegate not from the task itself. This page gives you a simple way to assign work to each AI "team member" based on their role:

- Content Marketer
- SEO Expert
- Copywriter
- Brand Designer
- Operations Manager
- Sales Strategist
- Launch Planner

You don't have to remember which prompts go where. You don't have to guess who handles what. You don't have to mentally organize your tasks. You simply fill in what each role needs to do today and let AI execute it. This makes delegation automatic. It makes clarity effortless. It keeps your business organized. And it trains your brain to think like a CEO rather than an overworked creator. This worksheet is your **team command center.**

HOW TO USE THIS WORKSHEET

Use this worksheet at the start of the week, during planning days, or whenever you feel mentally scattered and need a clear delegation plan.

1. Look at everything on your plate. List the tasks, ideas, content, systems, or problems you need to address.

2. Divide them by department. Fill in each section based on which AI "team member" should handle it. This step alone will eliminate 70% of your overwhelm.

3. Choose 1–2 tasks per category. You don't need to fill every box every day. You only need the tasks that matter this week.

4. Give all the tasks to AI using clear, simple commands. After filling out the sheet, write: **"Here are your assignments as my AI team. Complete each one in your designated role."** Copy the tasks from the sheet into your AI chat.

5. Let AI deliver everything for you. Workflows, templates, content, optimization, revenue plans, launch assets. All done *for you*, not by you.

6. Review, refine, save, and implement. This becomes your weekly automation, content, and operations engine.

WHY THIS WORKS

✓ It organizes your brain.

✓ It organizes your business.

✓ It turns mental chaos into delegation clarity.

✓ It prevents you from doing tasks that aren't yours anymore.

✓ It keeps you in your CEO identity daily.

And most importantly: **It eliminates the question "Where do I even start?"
because you let your team start FOR you.**

Content Marketer — What I need AI to create:

_____

_____

SEO Expert — What I need AI to optimize:

_____

_____

Copywriter — What I need AI to write:

_____

_____

Brand Designer — What I need AI to define or template:

_____

_____

Operations Manager — Systems or workflows AI should build:

_____

_____

Sales Strategist — Revenue tasks AI can take over:

_____

_____

Launch Planner — What AI must prepare for my next launch:

_____

_____

_____

WORKSHEET:
BUILD MY FIRST AUTOMATION

Your first step into a business that runs without you.

This worksheet is designed to walk you into your *first real automation*. The one that finally removes a repetitive, draining task from your life and replaces it with ease, consistency, and time freedom.

Most women don't automate because they think it's "technical" or "complicated."
It's not. Automation always begins with one simple question: **"What do I keep doing over and over that I should NEVER be doing manually again?"**

Once you identify the task, AI will build the workflow, write the steps, create the triggers, and architect the system. Your only job is to choose the first domino. The one task that creates the biggest relief.

This worksheet teaches you how to do that. This is the moment your business crosses from hustle… into systems. From survival mode… into scalability. From "I have to do everything myself"… into "I delegate like a CEO."

HOW TO USE THIS WORKSHEET

1. Identify the most repetitive, soul-sucking task.

This could be:
– Writing the same kind of email
– Manually posting content
– Sending onboarding messages
– Sorting files
– Tracking tasks
– Copy/pasting anything
– Editing the same template every time
– Answering the same questions across platforms

Write the specific task in the first box.

2. Write how often it happens.

Daily?
Multiple times a day?
Weekly?
This helps you understand the actual energy drain.

3. Write the time it steals each week.

Be honest. If it's 15 minutes a day, that's 1 hour and 45 minutes weekly. If it's a 30-minute task you avoid for days, that's mental energy on top of time. This number is your **automation ROI.**

4. Describe what it would look like fully automated.

Not the "how." Just the outcome.

Examples:
– "Content gets scheduled without me touching it."
– "Emails go out automatically when someone downloads the freebie."
– "My client onboarding happens instantly."
– "My files organize themselves."
– "My weekly blog post gets written, formatted, and SEO'd automatically."

This helps AI understand the vision.

5. Write the prompt you'll give AI.

This is the command that activates everything. It can be simple:

✓ "Build an automation that handles ___ for me from start to finish."

✓ "Automate this entire process: _____."

✓ "Create a hands-off workflow for _____ and tell me how to implement it."

AI will do the heavy lifting.

6. Describe what life feels like with this off your plate.

This is the energetic anchor. Examples:
– "My mind feels spacious."
– "I have my mornings back."
– "My business feels lighter."
– "I feel like a CEO again."
– "I have time to create, not maintain."

This emotional clarity helps you choose the *right* task, not just the easiest one.

WHY THIS WORKS

✓ You're choosing ONE automation — not ten.

✓ You feel immediate relief, proof, momentum.

✓ You begin trusting AI as your systems partner.

✓ You build confidence with delegation.

✓ You stop wasting hours on tasks that should never touch your hands.

This worksheet turns automation from an idea… into an identity shift.

What Repetitive Task Drains Me the Most?

_____

How Often I Do It:

_____

Time It Steals Weekly:

_____

What This Would Look Like Fully Automated:

_____

Prompt I Will Ask AI to Build This Automation:

_____

What My Life Feels Like When This Is Off My Plate:

_____

_____

WORKSHEET:
AI SOP CREATOR

Turn any task into a clean, repeatable, hands-off system.

This worksheet transforms any recurring task in your business into a fully documented, step-by-step SOP (Standard Operating Procedure) that AI builds *for you*. If you've never created an SOP before, here's the truth:

You don't need to know the steps.
You don't need to be organized.
You don't need to understand systems.
You just need to tell AI what the task is and what you're trying to achieve.

AI will break it down, tighten it, simplify it, optimize it, and turn it into a clean process you (or AI, or a VA) can execute perfectly every time.

This worksheet helps you identify the task…
clarify the outcome…
and give AI the instructions it needs to build the SOP from scratch.

This is how you go from
"I'm doing everything manually,"
to
"My business runs because my systems run."

HOW TO USE THIS WORKSHEET

1. Write the task you want SOP'd.

Choose something that:
– you repeat constantly
– you procrastinate on
– you wish someone else could do
– drains your energy
– must be done the *same way every time*

Examples:
- Posting content
- Email sequences
- Client onboarding
- Filing and organizing digital assets
- Updating product listings
- Scheduling social posts
- Editing video clips
- Writing weekly newsletters

Pick **one** task.

2. Define the outcome.

You're not describing the steps only the end result.

Examples:
✓ "A finished blog post ready to publish each week."
✓ "My clients receive onboarding emails automatically."
✓ "My content is posted across all platforms consistently."
✓ "My TikToks are edited in my brand style."

AI needs to know what "done" looks like.

3. Write the steps you *think* it takes.

This is not about perfection, it's about clarity. You're simply giving AI your best guess.

Even if you write messy, incomplete steps, AI will:
– correct them
– add missing pieces
– reorganize them
– streamline them
– turn everything into a clean standard operating procedure

Just give it a rough roadmap.

4. Explain what you struggle with.

This is where AI optimizes the workflow around your weaknesses.

Examples:
– "I forget steps."
– "I jump around instead of following an order."
– "It takes me too long."
– "I overthink everything."
– "I don't know what the first step should be."
– "I lose documents or links."

AI will build a smarter process based on your challenges.

5. Write the instructions AI will use to generate your SOP.

These are your "build commands."

Examples:
✓ "Turn this into a clean, step-by-step SOP I can follow or delegate."
✓ "Make this process easier, faster, and more efficient."
✓ "Rewrite this workflow so a beginner could follow it with no confusion."
✓ "Systematize this task and turn it into a repeatable SOP."

This tells AI what kind of SOP you want: simple, beginner-friendly, automated, efficient, or structured.

Why This Worksheet Matters

Because once a task is written as an SOP:

✓ You no longer have to reinvent the process every time
✓ Your brain stops burning energy thinking through steps
✓ You can delegate it to AI or a VA instantly
✓ You gain time, clarity, consistency
✓ Your business feels like it has *infrastructure,* not chaos

This is how you move from a solo creator…

to a woman with a functioning internal team.

Task I Want SOP'd:

_____

Outcome of This Task:

_____

Steps I *think* it takes (AI will refine):

1. _____

2. _____

3. _____

What I Struggle with in This Task:

_____

AI Instructions to Build the SOP for Me:

_____

_____

CLOSING NOTE

This is Where You Become Unstoppable

Step 8 is not about doing more.
It's about *never doing the wrong things again.*

This step gives you your time back.
Your sanity back.
Your body back.
Your life back.
Your power back.

You are not meant to run your empire alone.

You are meant to lead it,
supported, resourced, and elevated
by the systems and AI that hold you.

This is how you scale without collapsing.
This is how you grow without pressure.
This is how you build a business that supports your life
instead of consuming it.

This is where you rise.
This is where your empire becomes inevitable.

www.ingramcontent.com/pod-product-compliance
Lightning Source LLC
Chambersburg PA
CBHW081655120626
46550CB00010B/2909